This book is dedicated to my wife Carolyn. Caz has been my rock throughout my writing journey. From my previous book, *51 Shirts*, to this one, she has stood by me every step of the way.

When doubt crept in, mainly around the keeper shirts I had in the collection, Carolyn was there, encouraging me and reminding me of why I wanted to write the book. Her positivity is contagious, which certainly helped when I suffered the occasional bout of writer's block!

Her editing skills are legendary at least in the Young household! She manages to turn my words into almost coherent paragraphs and sentences.

Cazzo, you've made this entire process not just enjoyable, but a pleasure. Thank you, my fellow Jambo.

During the writing of this book, my dad and hero Alex Young sadly passed away. He was a Hearts supporter through thick and thin for 70 years. He passed on his passion to me, and I will for ever be grateful for everything he taught me and for his love and support. He will be missed by everyone who knew him. I loved sharing everything with him and know that he is still part of the next chapter in this story. Forever Hearts.

WE'RE IN SAFE HANDS

Pitch Publishing Ltd
9 Donnington Park
85 Birdham Road
Chichester
West Sussex
PO20 7AJ

Email: info@pitchpublishing.co.uk
Web: www.pitchpublishing.co.uk

First published by Pitch Publishing 2025.

1

A CIP catalogue record for this book is available from the British Library.

13-digit ISBN: 9781801509282
Design, photography and typesetting by Olner Pro Sport Media. Visit www.olnerpsm.co.uk
Printed in India by Replika Press, India

This book is printed on environmentally friendly paper.

GRANT YOUNG

WE'RE IN SAFE HANDS

HEART OF MIDLOTHIAN

FOREWORD BY JAMIE MACDONALD

pitch

CONTENTS

ŪKIO
BANKAS

FOREWORD

JAMIE MACDONALD

It's accurate to say that Heart of Midlothian is in my blood. Having had the complete joy of being welcomed into this football family some 25 years ago, I could never have known the journey I would embark on, experiencing the highest of highs to the sadness of leaving in 2014.

Winning the Scottish Cup on that special day, 19 May 2012, is a moment I'll never forget. It was an honour to walk out wearing the badge, and the support and love that I felt is something that will remain with me for evermore.

It was that momentous occasion that eventually led to my introduction to the wonderful Hearts fan and author that is Grant Young.

When I was invited along to the *51 Shirts* book launch at Tynecastle, I was totally intrigued. The concept of a book about the history of football shirts worn by Hearts greats like Alex Young back in 1959 and Henry Smith in 1993, up to more recent legends like my 2012 team-mates Rudi Skácel and the greatly missed Marius Žaliūkas is something that I knew so many could relate to. Grant even included my striking yellow and black Wonga number and, in an instant, I was transported back to that night at White Hart Lane where unbeknown to me, I'd save a penalty from someone who is now one of the world's most prolific strikers in Harry Kane. With each shirt telling its own story, fellow fans and players were able to revisit a particular moment in time. I flicked through the pages in awe. I reflected on the shirts I recognised from my own Hearts career and could relate to stadiums, scores, the fans, the songs and chants that filled the air. I then realised what Grant had penned was something that would be special to so many.

The success of *51 Shirts* has inevitably paved the way for Grant's new book, *We're in Safe Hands*, which is particularly special to me in that it cements the 'Goalkeepers Union' mantra and recognises the beauty of the lone man between the sticks. I find it somewhat fitting that I've since returned 'Home' to Hearts in 2024 in a player mentor role with the B team. It is a position that I relish and thrive on working with the next generation of Hearts players each day. When Grant asked me to do my bit, it was an honour and a no-brainer for me.

Hearts Forever.

Jamie MacDonald

INTRODUCTION

I have always had an admiration for goalkeepers. They are a crucial part of the team, but behind the gloves lies a world of solitude and pressure. Goalkeepers often carry the weight of victory and defeat on their shoulders. In these modern times, keepers are always under the microscope and are quickly judged for the slightest of errors. The flip side of that is the adoration shown from the crowd when they showcase their agility or bravery in that split second when they secure a result with the flick of a wrist or a crazy act of selflessness.

As a young fan, I stood in awe watching Henry Smith defy gravity. His acrobatics were more than saves; they were magic moments woven into the fabric of our team's history. For me, he encapsulated a goalkeeper. Each season, I would witness moments of brilliance, craziness, the odd mistake, and a persona that was both introverted and extroverted!

During our pre-match pub chatter, the best save by a Hearts goalkeeper will occasionally come up for discussion. For me, it hasn't changed in over 30 years. Henry's save against Tommy Coyne in a league match against Celtic is the most incredible feat of agility I have ever witnessed. With Celtic a goal up, Coyne got on the end of a cross and cleverly headed it towards the corner of the goal. Henry, going the wrong way, twisted in mid-air and somehow got fingers to it to claw the ball over the bar. That save reinvigorated Hearts to go on and win 3-1. Unbelievable! Since then, I have had the privilege of seeing some incredible keepers arrive in Gorgie, including the French giant Gilles Rousset, Antti Niemi, Jamie MacDonald, Neil Alexander, Jon McLaughlin, Zander Clark and of course, arguably the best keeper that Scotland has ever produced, Craig Gordon. I come from a long line of Hearts supporters, and it would be remiss of me not to mention keepers that my dad and grandad cheered for from the terraces like Jack Harkness, Jimmy Brown, Gordon Marshall, Willie Duff, and of course, Jim Cruickshank. There have been many others that have made cameo appearances down Gorgie way but, nonetheless, they have still left an indelible mark on the club's history.

Over the 20-odd years of collecting mainly Hearts match-worn shirts, I have always made a point of picking up keeper shirts whenever one that catches my eye becomes available. In all honesty, keeper shirts are harder to find due to the scarcity factor. By that, I mean there are always ten outfield players and several substitutes, but with keepers, there is only one on the pitch and usually one on the bench. It's also clear that keepers love swapping their shirts with their opposite numbers, making it even more difficult for collectors. I am extremely lucky that my collection includes an array of Hearts and international goalkeeper shirts worn by some of the names I have already mentioned. Naturally, like any other shirt collector, I am always trying to track down shirts that have been worn by my heroes. The thrill of the chase is something that will never abate and that's why I am continually and obsessively following up every lead that comes my way if it means I end up being the privileged custodian of another piece of Heart of Midlothian history.

This publication gives me a rare opportunity to showcase and share my collection of keeper shirts. It gives you the chance to step back in time and remember who you were with and how you felt when recalling some amazing matches, incredible saves, memorable individual performances and highlights from eye-catching seasons. Perhaps there are some players whose time may have been fleeting, but you will never forget that penalty save or crazy warm-up routine. The book also documents how styles and designs have changed through the decades. How shirts have moved from the very traditional and sometimes muted templates of the 70s and early 80s to the outlandish designs of the 90s, right up to the tighter and sleeker shirts of today.

Admiral
GK

SCOTLAND'S NUMBER ONE

2005/06 – 2024/25

CRAIG GORDON

This chapter was the hardest by far to write. How on earth could I cover Craig Gordon's Hearts career in one chapter? It's quite an undertaking, but I will try my best.

On 3 March 2001, Roddy McKenzie made his first appearance of the season as regular keeper Antti Niemi had to miss the game due to a stomach virus. This meant that an 18-year-old Craig Gordon got his first experience of first-team football as he took his place on the bench at Ibrox against Rangers.

The following season, on 6 October 2002, at the age of 19 years and seven months, Craig was given his debut by Craig Levein against Livingston at Almondvale. The game ended in a 1-1 draw. McKenzie had failed a test on a thigh strain and young Gordon repaid his manager's faith with an excellent display, including a full-length dive to keep out a well-struck shot from Gary Bollan. Craig received the Man of the Match trophy from the Livingston fans that day, a trophy which is still highly valued amongst his large haul of honours. He would make one further appearance that season, in the Scottish Cup defeat to Falkirk at Brockville.

He would oust Finnish keeper Tepi Moilanen for the number one spot during the following season, 2003/04. From that point onwards, he never looked back. His performances that season would see him win the Scottish Football Writers' Association (SFWA) Young Player of the Year award as well as being named SPL Young Player of the Year. His excellent form would also see the 21-year-old make his Scotland debut alongside team-mate Steven Pressley in a 4-1 win against Trinidad and Tobago at Easter Road on 30 May 2004.

Craig became a legend in 2005/06 when Hearts finished second in the league and won the Scottish Cup. With the score 1-1 after 120 minutes, the game went to the dreaded penalty shoot-out. Hearts triumphed 4-2. Craig played a pivotal role by saving Derek Townsley's penalty, while Gavin Skelton's effort hit the crossbar. Steven Pressley, Robbie Neilson, Rudi Skácel, and Michal Pospíšil deftly converted their penalties to secure the victory; a nerve-racking experience for all involved.

Gordon was inducted into Hearts' Hall of Fame in 2007, becoming the youngest player to receive the honour.

In August 2007, Gordon moved to Sunderland for £9m, a then British record transfer fee for a goalkeeper. He later joined Celtic in 2014, winning multiple Scottish Premiership titles, League Cups and Scottish Cups before returning to Hearts in 2020.

Gordon's return to Tynecastle was nothing short of spectacular: he helped Hearts win the Championship title and secure third place in the 2021/22 Premiership. His performances earned him a third SFWA Player of the Year award, making him the only player in history to win it three times.

On Boxing Day 2022, he suffered a double leg break in a sickening clash with Dundee United striker Steven Fletcher at Tannadice. It wasn't the first time that Craig had faced a career-threatening injury either. When playing with Sunderland, he suffered a serious knee injury that required extensive rehabilitation and surgery. This setback led to him being released by Sunderland in 2012, as the club believed he might not recover sufficiently to continue playing at the top level. After what happened at Dundee United, he was sidelined for over nine months as he underwent rehabilitation and recovery. Despite the severity of the injury, Gordon made a remarkable comeback to football with Hearts in October 2023, playing in a behind-closed-doors game against Spartans. Then, on 20 January 2024, 392 days after suffering the double leg break, he was back in the starting 11, against Spartans in the fourth round of

hummel
ŪKIO BANKAS

BANK OF SCOTLAND
PREMIERLEAGUE

the Scottish Cup at Ainslie Park, with Hearts winning 2-1. Many had thought Craig wouldn't recover from the injury. However, many underestimated the drive, determination and sheer willpower that he possesses. He was back in business.

There are so many amazing statistics and record-breaking facts associated with the Hearts legend.

When Hearts drew 0-0 with Dunfermline at East End Park in the Championship on 3 April 2021, it would be the start of nine consecutive games without conceding a goal. Gordon was in goal for all the games and surpassed Jon McLaughlin's previous record of eight clean sheets.

On 15 November 2021, Scotland defeated Denmark 2-0 in a 2022 World Cup qualifier. Craig played in the game which meant he became the most-capped player in Hearts' history, having earned 33 Scotland caps while playing for the club. He surpassed former skipper and team-mate Steven Pressley, who was on 32 caps.

On 4 May 2022, Craig became the first player to be named SFWA Footballer of the Year on three different occasions: 2005/06 with Hearts, 2014/15 with Celtic and again with Hearts in 2021/22.

When Craig recorded 20 clean sheets in 2021/22, he slotted into fifth place behind another Hearts legend, Henry Smith, who held the top four slots with 1991/92 (25 clean sheets), 1987/88 (24) and 1986/87 and 1988/89 (21 both times).

Craig won his 74th cap for Scotland in a 2-1 defeat against Turkey in an international friendly on 16 November 2022. It meant he recorded a landmark 700th senior appearance.

When Craig started against Viktoria Plzeň on 22 August 2024 in the Czech Republic, it meant he had made more European appearances for Hearts than any other player, moving ahead of Henry Smith and Steven Pressley.

On 7 December 2024, Craig started in a 2-0 win against Dundee at Tynecastle. It was his 100th clean sheet for the club.

When Craig took the field against Ross County on 15 March 2025 at Tynecastle, it was his 324th appearance, and he had also been an unused sub 76 times. He had therefore appeared on the club's team

sheet for the 400th time. This tally started when he sat on the bench against Rangers at Ibrox on 3 March 2001. Quite a remarkable record and some stunning facts.

He was recently asked at a fan event if he could have played in any game that another goalkeeper had played in, what would it be? Without hesitation, he said it would be to replace Jamie MacDonald in the 2012 Scottish Cup Final. He was there with family and friends, and as a Hearts fan, it was an unforgettable day. He also loved the fact that he played a small part in the 1998 Scottish Cup Final at Parkhead when Hearts defeated Rangers 2-1. He was asked to take part in a penalty shoot-out at half-time. Again, as a fan it was a day to remember.

He went on to talk about two keepers he admired. Growing up, he thought Henry Smith was an amazing role model as well as a tremendous goalkeeper. Craig had a special mention for his Sunderland team-mate Simon Mignolet. Simon was brought in as Gordon's understudy, with Craig acknowledging that the competition made him an even better keeper. Craig left the Black Cats in 2012, and Mignolet would leave a season later, joining Liverpool for £9m.

Craig was asked if he could pick out a favourite save. To my surprise, it was a very recent one in a 1-0 win against Motherwell on 2 January 2024. He pulled off a magnificent stop to deny Jack Vale's point-blank header in stoppage time to ensure the three points stayed in Gorgie. He somehow managed to push the header over the bar and quite rightly celebrated as if he had just scored the winner in the dying seconds. A quite stunning save.

Craig has made so many incredible saves for the club that it would be virtually impossible to pick a top three, and I'm sure every fan could compile a different list. I am going to give you my top three, but in no particular order:

Hearts 2 Motherwell 1, 27 August 2005

Hearts had just about seen out their fifth successive victory to start the season, which would eventually stretch to eight, but only thanks to some late heroics from Gordon.

Rudi Skácel and Edgaras Jankauskas had the Men in Maroon 2-0 up with 20 minutes to go before Ritchie Foran pulled one back for the Steelmen from the spot.

In the third minute of stoppage time, David Clarkson struck a volley from the penalty spot as sweetly as he could, destined for the net, only for Gordon to show unfathomable reactions to get across and tip it wide with two hands.

Hibernian 2 Hearts 2, 15 October 2006

It looked like an uphill struggle for Hearts when they found themselves 2-0 down inside 15 minutes after quickfire strikes from Merouane Zemmama and Chris Killen.

However, as was quite often the case, Hibs keeper Zibi Małkowski handed his arch rivals a lifeline, inexplicably coming for and getting nowhere near a cross which allowed Lithuanian striker Andrius Velička to head home from 18 yards.

Velička struck again on 72 minutes with a snap shot that went in at the near post. This sparked celebrations in the away end.

The Hibs support must have thought they'd won it late on when a deep cross slung into the box was met by 6ft 7in skipper Rob Jones. The centre-back rose and planted a header back across goal that looked for all the world to be heading for the far corner. Gordon, however, showed stunning reactions and agility to leap to his left and claw the ball away from goal and deny Hibs what would surely have been a late winner. A truly unbelievable stop!

Hearts 0 Sparta Prague 2, 14 September 2006

Although Hearts' hopes of progressing to the Europa League group stages were effectively extinguished on a rainy night at Murrayfield, one man was still trying his best to perform at the highest standard: Craig Gordon. Daniel Kolář's drive had put the Czechs ahead, and they were to be denied a second by Gordon's heroics when he produced an outrageous triple save. The stop from Libor Došek's initial shot was decent enough with his legs, before denying Kolář and Ludovic Sylvestre from the rebounds. It highlighted Gordon's determination, agility and athleticism. A sequence of saves never to be forgotten for those who witnessed it.

Stellar
Omada

Craig Gordon exemplifies everything that is good about a football player. A class act, a class goalkeeper and a superb ambassador for Heart of Midlothian Football Club. His journey from a young bench-warmer to a celebrated legend is a testament to his talent, determination and unwavering dedication. Personally, it's been a pleasure to have been around to watch his career go from strength to strength, from first seeing him play at Brockville in the Scottish Cup in January 2003 right up to the 2024/25 season and still watching in awe as he pulls off stunning saves game after game. A true Hearts great.

The first shirt was worn by Craig against Motherwell in a 0-0 draw at Fir Park on 12 April 2025. The quite stunning design features a white base with a multicolour graphic running across the sleeves and the top of the shirt. The design is described as a modernisation of the club's early colours (white, blue and red), giving it an abstract and striking appearance. The design choice reflects a trend in modern kits to blend heritage with contemporary aesthetics, particularly for goalkeeper outfits, which often serve as a visual contrast to the team's primary colours, meaning the designers have room to play with the colours and graphics of the shirt.

It's part of Umbro's collection, celebrating the company's 100th anniversary. Personally, it's my favourite keeper shirt that Hearts have produced since the white adidas shirt from the 2014/15 season.

The second shirt is in my top five Hearts goalkeeper shirts and was worn by Craig in 2005/06 and is instantly recognisable, as he wore the same version in the 2006 Scottish Cup Final against Gretna.

The shirt is predominantly black with white detailing. The standout on the shirt is Hummel's iconic chevron patterns on the sleeves, a hallmark of their designs during this era. The front features the logo of Ukio Bankas, a Lithuanian bank tied to the club's then-owner, Vladimir Romanov. The Hummel logo is prominently displayed, reflecting the brand's brief return to Hearts in the 2000s. The back features Craig Gordon's name set and number. For me this is a timeless design classic that could be brought back for any new season.

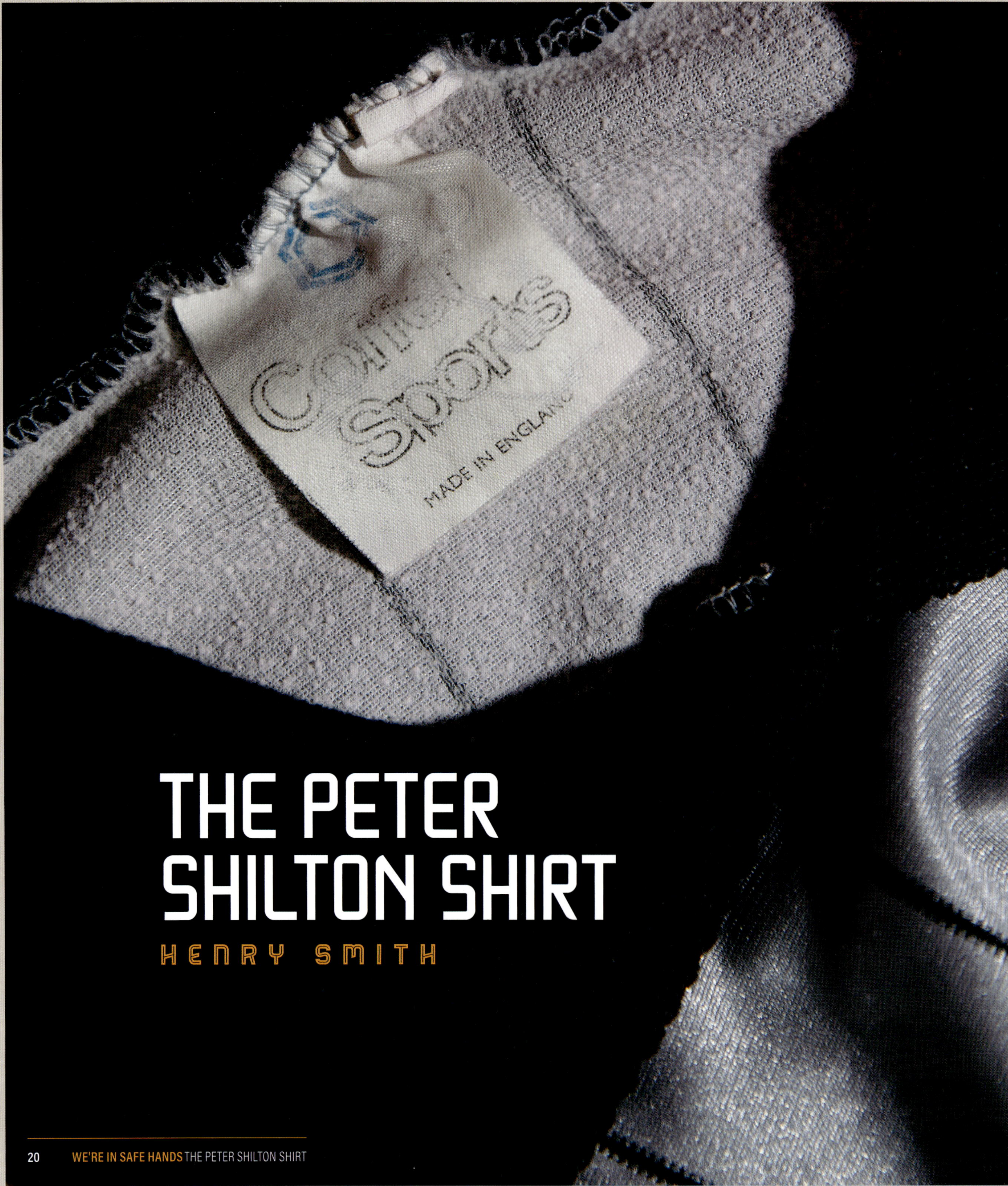

THE PETER SHILTON SHIRT

HENRY SMITH

1982/83

The 1982/83 season was pivotal for Hearts both on and off the field. On the pitch, it was out with the old and in with the new: the club had worn the iconic Umbro shirt, which featured the famous double diamonds, from 1977/78 through to the end of 1981/82. The keeper shirt was the traditional yellow with the alternative blue shirt being worn on occasion. However, 1982/83 would see a huge shift in style.

A new style of shirt made its debut in the friendly against Sheffield United at Tynecastle on Wednesday, 4 August 1982 in front of a crowd of 3,500. Or did it?

A sponsorless version of the new yellow keeper kit was worn by Henry Smith at Rugby Park at the end of 1981/82, not that the Hearts fans among the bumper 10,000 crowd would have been paying much attention to these minor details. They had come along to see if Hearts could win to keep their promotion hopes alive by securing the points. The 0-0 result meant Hearts would have all to play for the following week at Tynecastle against Motherwell but ultimately they just fell short in a 1-0 defeat. The yellow shirt can be clearly identified from the game highlights on YouTube.

Back to 1982/83 and Umbro would produce two keeper shirts for the season: a home yellow-bodied, black-sleeved, matching collared effort worn with black shorts and an away grey-bodied shirt with black sleeves and matching collar. On each shirt, the Umbro logo appeared left of centre and the Hearts crest on the right. During the season, Henry was seen wearing both these versions with and without the Alexanders sponsor.

THE TWIST IN THIS STORY IS THAT THE SILVER SHIRT WAS NOT PRODUCED BY UMBRO – IT WAS MANUFACTURED BY THE ENGLISH SPORTS COMPANY COFFERS.

However, it appears that the shirt Henry preferred to wear was silver with black pinstripes and matching black cuffs and V-neck collar. Interestingly, it had no manufacturer logo or Hearts crest! So, what was the background surrounding this shirt? I had always assumed it was an Umbro template or perhaps a sample that was sent to the club by Umbro and Henry tried it out and liked it. Rumour even has it that Hearts liked the silver keeper shirt so much that the ill-fated silver away kit was born from that very production.

The twist in this story is that the silver shirt was not produced by Umbro – it was manufactured by the English sports company Coffers. Back in the early 80s, Coffers had secured the services of England international goalkeeper Peter Shilton, who wore Coffers shirts from 1981 to 1983. Perhaps Coffers were keen to promote their shirts in Scotland. Did Hearts receive a few samples and Henry ended up wearing them?

This shirt has a great story behind it in terms of how it ended up in my collection. Club ambassador, former player, captain and Hearts supporter Gary Locke gave me the shirt. How did he acquire it? Gary went to all the games with his dad and brothers on the Bonnyrigg Hearts supporters' bus. As a family, they

RUMOUR HAS IT THAT HEARTS LIKED THE SILVER KEEPER SHIRT SO MUCH THAT THE ILL-FATED SILVER AWAY KIT WAS BORN FROM THAT VERY PRODUCTION.

made the trip to the penultimate match of 1982/83, away to Dumbarton on 7 May 1983. A win would see Hearts promoted to the Premier League. Two superb goals from a young John Robertson in a devastating first-half display, followed by a goal apiece from Derek O'Connor and Gary Mackay in the second half, saw Hearts secure top-flight football for 1983/84. At the final whistle, there were jubilant scenes on and off the pitch. Many fans invaded the turf and celebrated with the players. Gary was one of those fans, helped on to the pitch by his dad. He chanced his luck by running up to Henry Smith and asking for his shirt. Much to Gary's surprise, Henry duly obliged. Little did they both know that they would end up team-mates in years to come. Gary kindly offered the shirt to me and was delighted that the family's story could be shared.

Shirts from this period are very rare as the players usually survived with two to four for the whole season and very rarely got to keep them.

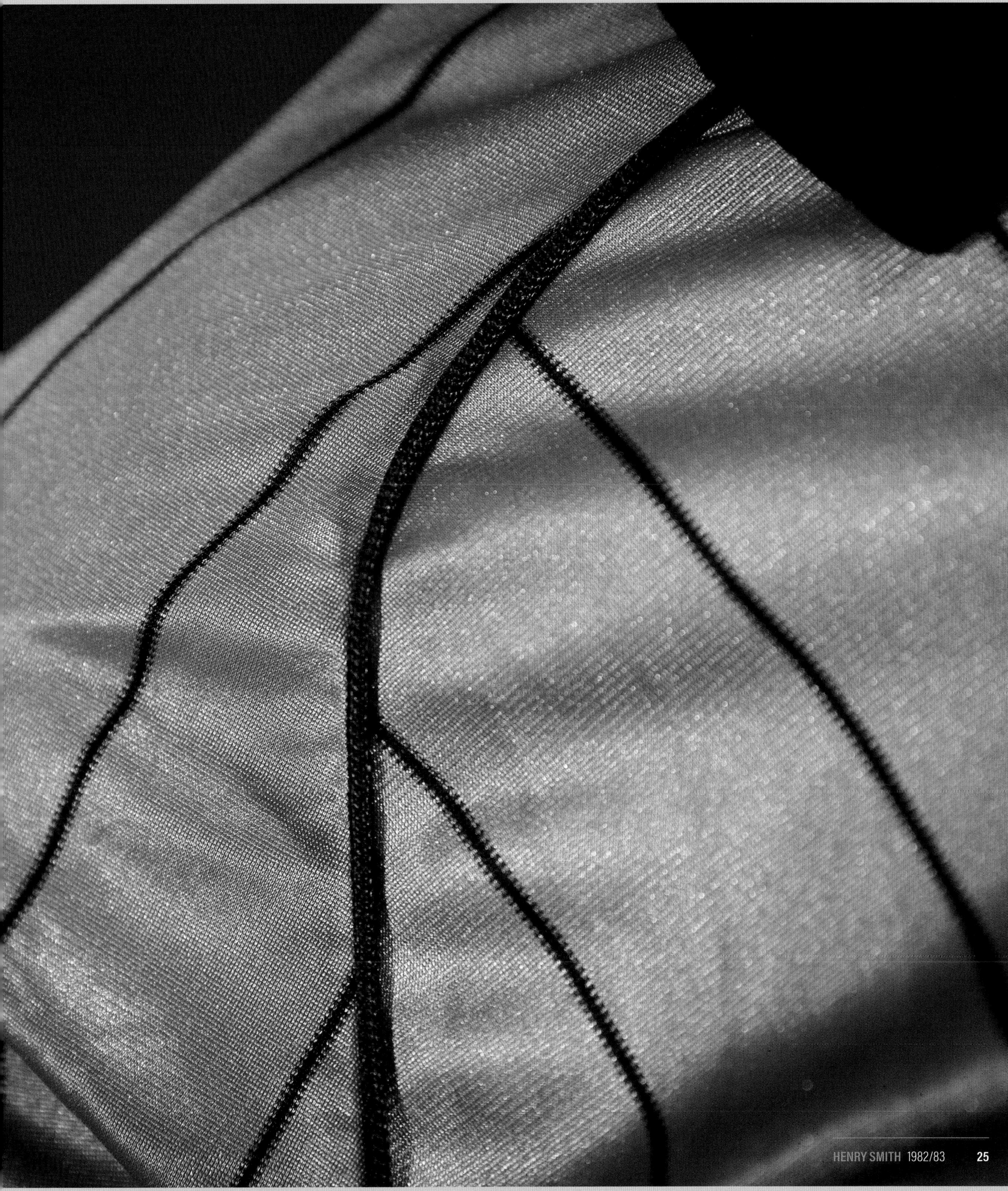

THE SILVERWARE RUSH

GORDON MARSHALL

The pre-season paper talk in July 1956 was that Tommy Walker was on the hunt for a new goalkeeper after regular number one Willie Duff received his call-up papers for national service. It left the manager with only one keeper at Tynecastle, Wilson Brown, who Walker trusted to make the step up.

Walker confirmed this by handing the 21-year-old the first peg in the dressing room. It was felt in the press that he still had to go out and source another keeper and Dunfermline's Joe Mackin was the hot favourite. The move never transpired. At the beginning of August, Hearts moved for the untested Gordon Marshall. He joined the club with two other former local juvenile side Balgreen Rovers players, George Summers and Billy Higgins. Gordon would come out the blocks quickly, featuring for Hearts' reserves against city rivals Hibs on 14 August in the Reserve League Cup in a 2-2 draw at Easter Road.

He then made his first senior appearance for Hearts in a friendly against Newcastle, a team he would later sign for. Remarkably, Gordon was only 17 years and two months old when he walked onto St James' Park in front of a crowd of 23,000 in September 1956. The result was a 2-1 win for an understrength Hearts against a Newcastle team that included the legendary Jackie Milburn. It also saw the Magpies beaten at home for the first time that season. Gordon was given a special mention by Jimmy Cowe in the *Edinburgh Dispatch* where it was written, 'A pat on the back for Marshall who was given a baptism of fire but did well.'

A mere two months later he would make his senior competitive debut for Hearts in a 3-2 win at Tynecastle against Kilmarnock on 17 November 1956. Wilson Brown had been bothered for several weeks with a pulled muscle and young Gordon was called upon. Post-match, the *Sunday Post* ran with the headline 'I raise my hat to the Tynecastle toddlers'. This referred to Tommy Walker giving the opportunity to the youngsters at the club. Half a dozen reserve players took to the field, one behind another, which may well have been the youngest ever XI to represent the club in a league match. Seventeen-year-old Gordon and the whole forward line (except for Jimmy Wardhaugh) were eligible to play for their national under-23 side: Jim McFadzean (18), Alex Young (19), Johnny Hamilton (21) and Ian Crawford (22). Kilmarnock had whacked Aberdeen the week before but 'the toddlers' hammered the men from Ayrshire. With Hearts winning 3-2, they battered the Killie goal with shots raining in on ex-Tynecastle keeper Jimmy Brown from all angles. The reporter for the *Sunday Post* was the former Hearts and Scotland goalkeeper Jack Harkness. The Wembley Wizard knew a thing or two about goalkeeping. In the same article he wrote that '17-year-old Marshall had immense promise written all

over'. How right he was. It can't be overstated how well Marshall dealt with the pressure, as only three months earlier he had been playing juvenile football.

Gordon would go on to make 11 appearances in 1956/57. He would then become the first-choice keeper from 1957/58 through to 1962/63, reaching an incredible 267 competitive appearances just two months before his 24th birthday. In his seven years at Tynecastle, Marshall etched his way into history by collecting five domestic medals. Notably, he missed only three matches during the 1957/58 league-winning campaign and just one match when Hearts secured a league and League Cup double in 1959/60.

When winning the League Cup against Partick Thistle he became the second-youngest player to win a domestic honour in the modern era, at the age of 19 years, three months and 18 days. Who pipped him to the youngest? The aptly named Alex Young who won the Scottish Cup against Celtic in 1956 aged 19 years, two months and 23 days. Not much in it!

He played his last game for Hearts at Fir Park against Motherwell on 11 May 1963, a 3-1 win. Ex-Hearts striker turned journalist Jimmy Wardhaugh broke the story of Gordon's departure to Newcastle in the *Scottish Daily Express*. The reported fee of £18,000 was a Scottish record for a goalkeeper. Marshall was asked about the shock move and said, 'The offer came right out of the blue; I had not asked for a transfer from Hearts. But this offer was one I could not refuse. The basic wage is higher than I could get at Tynecastle, and they [Newcastle] are helping me out with a house.' The terms were reported as £35 a week, a house at nominal rent, £4 win bonus, £2 a draw, a promotion bonus of £1,000 per player and a crowd bonus of £1 per thousand over 30,000 plus participation in the players' Benevolent Fund. The new contract would come in very handy for Gordon, who was about to be married the following week.

Marshall was born in Farnham, Surrey but he and his family moved to Edinburgh when he was three years old. His rise from juvenile football to the international game was complete when he was capped for England's under-23s, ironically playing against Scotland in a 4-4 draw on 2 March 1960. The England team included Bobby Charlton, George Cohen and Jimmy Greaves. Marshall always faced stiff competition for a starting place, competing with Gordon Banks, who would go on to win the World Cup, and Chelsea legend Peter Bonetti. He had at one point been selected for the Scotland under-23 team until his place of birth was pointed out to the selection committee.

Gordon was quite rightly inducted into the Heart of Midlothian Hall of Fame in 2016. I had the pleasure of spending an evening with him in the splendid Hearts Museum and thoroughly enjoyed his company as he recalled the glory years at Tynecastle. A true gentleman.

Although I don't have a match shirt from this Tynecastle great, the decision to write a chapter about him was an easy one. I have come close to obtaining one, but some shirts remain just out of reach. I live in hope! Gordon was one of my dad's heroes, and a book about Hearts goalkeepers would never feel complete without his story.

Gordon sadly passed away on 6 February 2025 at the age of 85.

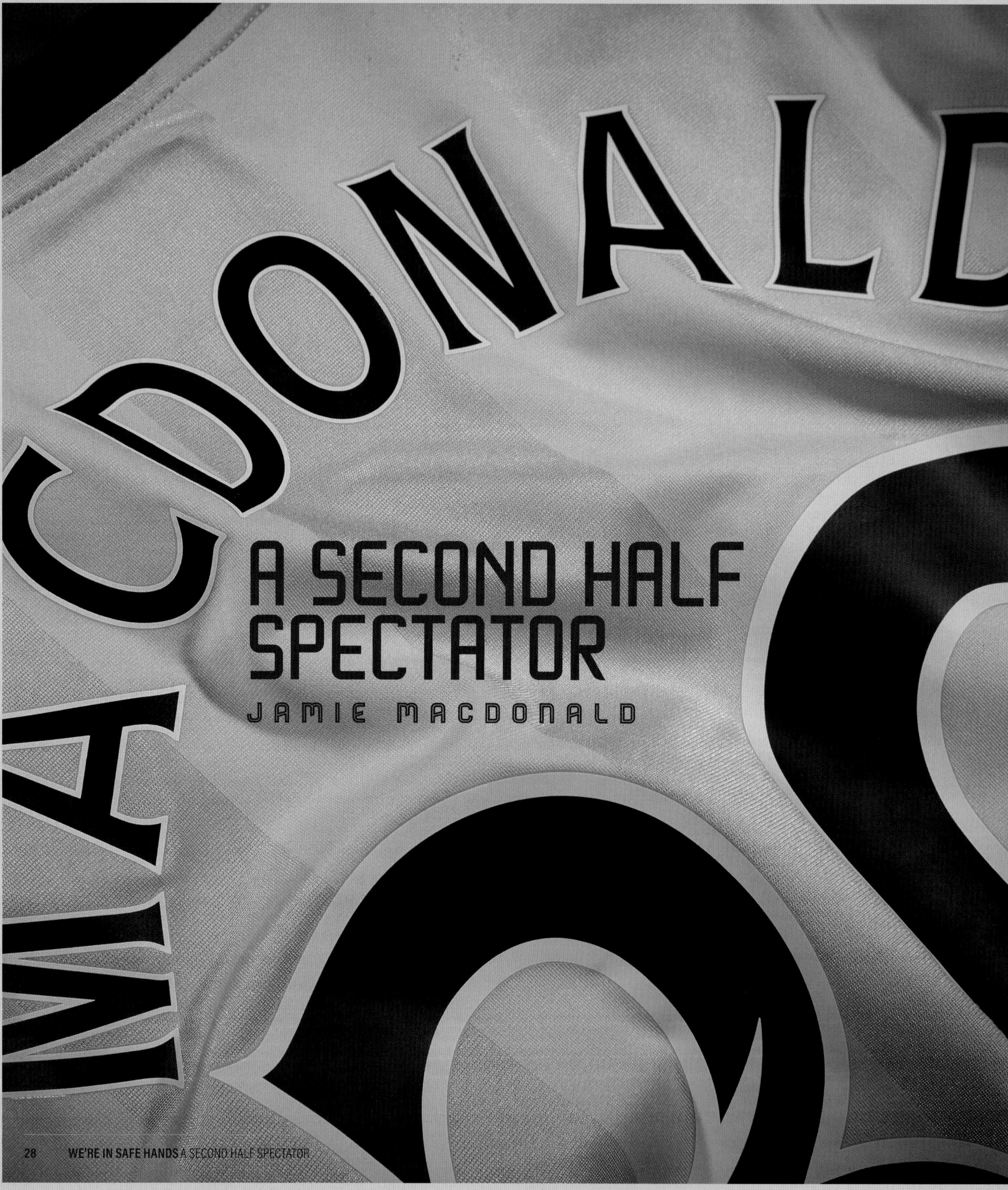

A SECOND HALF SPECTATOR

JAMIE MACDONALD

2004/05 – 2024/25

It's not at all contentious to say that Jamie MacDonald's role in the Scottish Cup Final against Hibs in 2012 was almost that of a spectator. However, it should never be understated the role he played to get Hearts to that point.

Jamie was not in manager Jim Jefferies's plans at the beginning of the 2011/12 season. The Slovakian international Marián Kello was the first-choice keeper, and when Jim departed the club on 1 August to be replaced by Paulo Sérgio, Sérgio also stuck with Kello as the number one. Jamie made a rare appearance away to Inverness on 10 September in a 1-1 draw. Although he made an error for the Inverness goal, he more than made up for it by keeping the home side at bay with a series of excellent saves. He kept his place in the team for league games until Kello was selected for the away trip to Dunfermline on 15 October. Marián remained a constant until the Scottish Cup fourth round tie against Auchinleck Talbot on 7 January 2012, when Jamie made a surprise return. It was later revealed in the press that Kello had refused a January move to Austria Vienna, and in true Vladimir Romanov style, he was frozen out of the team. Kello eventually left the club in April after being released early from his contract. This opened the door for Jamie, who played every game bar one after Kello's last appearance, against Inverness away on 21 January 2012. This included all ties in the Scottish Cup.

MacDonald had very little to do in the Auchinleck game and it was his opposite number Andy Leishman who received the plaudits after he denied Hearts on numerous occasions. Indeed, he played so well that for several weeks he was linked with a move to Tynecastle in various newspapers.

McCRAE'S BATTALION

'I WAS GIVEN A CHOICE BY THE KITMAN, 14, 6 OR 37 WHICH WAS MY OLD NUMBER AT CELTIC, AND I THOUGHT DO YOU KNOW WHAT, JUST GIVE ME NUMBER 4.'

Next up for the Men in Maroon was a home tie against St Johnstone on 5 February which ended 1-1 and required a replay at McDiarmid Park, a ground Hearts always found hard to negotiate. This one was no different and it took every ounce of dogged determination to get through the tie. Hearts negotiated a 2-1 victory after extra time, the winner coming from captain fantastic Marius Žaliūkas in the 117th minute, when he somehow bundled the ball home among a sea of bodies.

Fellow Premiership club St Mirren were up next, the first time that the home support got a good look at new signing Craig Beattie, who took the number 4 shirt. Before the game, Craig joked to the press about his choice of number, 'I was given a choice by the kitman, 14, 6 or 37 which was my old number at Celtic, and I thought do you know what, just give me number 4. A few forwards have worn random numbers, [Zinedine] Zidane wore number 5. I thought just chuck it out there and see what happens.' I think all Hearts fans would agree it was a good choice! In this game, he scored the equaliser and set up Rudi Skácel for the second. The game went to a replay even though MacDonald did his utmost to keep St Mirren out. With seven minutes to go, substitute Hasselbaink shot from a tight angle which Jamie blocked followed by a save from Gary Teale on the rebound. The ball was still loose, and after Nigel Hasselbaink knocked it across the six-yard area, Marius somehow directed the ball into his own net. Hearts were heading to Paisley for another replay.

St Mirren started the game very positively with attack after attack which MacDonald and his defence thwarted. He denied Hasselbaink a certain goal when he flew through the air and clawed back a shot that was destined for the top corner. Hasselbaink did get the better of him when after a stramash in the box he prodded home the loose ball. Much to the Saints' displeasure, referee Steve O'Reilly had spotted a handball in the box and awarded the penalty. St Mirren's Carey did little wrong when hitting the ball hard and low from the spot, but MacDonald at full stretch kept it out. St Mirren would rue that miss as within six minutes Jamie Hamill produced a sweet strike to make it 1-0. Skácel doubled the lead and made it nine goals against the Buddies in five matches. Against the backdrop of financial woes and non-payment of wages, Hearts had secured a money-spinning semi-final against Celtic, which will live long in the memory of any Hearts fan who bought a ticket. It will always be remembered for Craig Beattie's famous shirt-off celebration after he converted the penalty to give Hearts a 2-1 lead on 90 minutes. MacDonald again pulled off some crucial saves during the game as Celtic lay siege. He was at full stretch to deny Kris Commons and Charlie Mulgrew, but it was Hearts' day. The victory set up a Scottish Cup Final against city rivals Hibernian on 19 May. As the song goes 'Bring on the Hibees'.

The rest, as they say, is history.

Jamie made a total of 137 competitive appearances for the club and managed 33 clean sheets. He faced 23 penalties during his time at Hearts, saving four of them. Of course, the most famous penalty save was against the highly rated youngster Harry Kane during the return leg of the Europa League qualifier against Tottenham Hotspur on 25 August 2011. Kane, who was making his first Spurs appearance, earned a penalty when he was felled by Jamie. However, his firm effort was kept out well by Jamie who dived low to his right and prevented the debut goal. Jamie jokes that the save has taken

H·M
C
F
1874

Reebok
OFFICIAL TEAM MERCHANDISE
DEU 56
FRA 2XL
ITA 2XL 54
UK XL 46/48
USA XL 46/48

JAMIE MADE A TOTAL OF 137 COMPETITIVE APPEARANCES FOR THE CLUB AND MANAGED 33 CLEAN SHEETS. HE FACED 23 PENALTIES DURING HIS TIME AT HEARTS, SAVING FOUR OF THEM.

on much more of a legendary status as time has passed and as Kane has become one of the most prolific scorers in the modern game. Jamie also loves the fact that his kids have seen the save on YouTube and can't believe their dad has played against Kane and that he saved the penalty. Kudos for Jamie.

Cup legend Jamie's career has gone full circle as at the time of writing he was back at Hearts, joining the club's B team on a one-year deal in July 2024 after leaving Greenock Morton.

Speaking at the time to the club website, B team head coach Liam Fox said, 'First and foremost, it is great to have someone of Jamie's quality and standing within the game added to our group. Not only will he play a part on the pitch, but the learning he will provide to our younger players as well. He is keen to come back, keen to play and he knows he'll be held to the same standards as anyone else in the dressing room.

'It might seem like an older goalkeeper will block the pathway, but it's exactly the opposite. We have got two goalkeepers who have just turned full time, one 16 and the other about to turn 16, and we did not want to block their path. Jamie will help them find the time to develop and make that next step to the B team in the year to come.'

Jamie added, 'I am delighted. It is where I started my career and spent a large part of my life here. To come back and be involved with the B team is exciting for me. It's a different kind of challenge but one that involves helping the next generation of Hearts players to come through.'

I had the opportunity to catch up with Jamie on his return to the club, and we had a chat about his career. The main things that shone through were how much dedication and hard work he has put into his trade to reach the top. A work ethic that he got from both his parents, who encouraged him but also instilled the value of dedication at the same time. The mantra being if you are going to commit yourself to something, do it at 100 per cent with no regrets. He also had a special mention for John McGlynn, who had been his coach at Hearts when he was a youngster and later in his career managed him at Raith Rovers. Jamie recalled how John had at times seemed over-critical of aspects of his game, but as he got older, he realised he had been singled out for special attention as John saw the raw potential in the young keeper. Jamie added that he would imagine many young players would be grateful for the tutelage of the unassuming McGlynn.

He fondly recalled the 2012 Scottish Cup Final, calling out the importance of the penalty save against St Mirren and the numerous stops against Celtic in the semi-final. He laughed as he described being sick before the final against Hibs and then the pure joy at the sound of the final whistle.

When I asked Jamie about his finest save in a Hearts shirt, he laughed and said it was against Hibs at Easter Road on 27 April 2014. Hearts had a 2-1 lead thanks to two first-half goals from Callum Paterson. Jamie made an extraordinary save in the 95th minute from Hibs striker James Collins, which Bobby Madden ruled offside. Jamie joked that he had asked Bobby to give Hibs the corner as he knew the save would not officially count!

He was also very proud to receive the players' player of the year award at the end of the 2012/13 season.

umbro

H·M
C
F
1874

Finally, Jamie reflected on his role within the B team and hoped that he would help bring on another Scottish Cup-winning keeper. I do not think any Hearts fan would argue with that.

The first shirt is from the 2004/05 season. This is Jamie's shirt that he wore the first time he ever sat on the bench for the first team. Although he did not get any minutes, he was a substitute for the pre-season friendlies against Brechin City and Airdrie. It is a Reebok shirt in traditional yellow and black. A yellow body with white piping runs from shoulders to the elbows. The black sleeves run from the elbows to the black cuffs. The sleeves have a nice addition in that there are small hexagons entwined in them. The body also has vertical hexagons in the middle running from the stomach area to the neck. The hexagons get smaller and smaller as they reach the neck. The back bears Jamie's first squad number, which is 29.

The second shirt is from the 2010/11 season. It's Jamie's bench-worn Remembrance shirt from the 2-1 win against St Johnstone on 13 November at McDiarmid Park. I included this shirt as it's another yellow and black classic but also features stunning embroidery work with the Contalmaison cairn appearing front and centre of the shirt, with a reference to McCrae's Battalion below the cairn. The poppy appears on the left-hand side of the shirt under the club crest, with the word 'Remember' in maroon below. With a yellow body and black sleeves, it's a simple but pleasing design, but what makes this shirt pop even more for me is the maroon 'Ukio Bankas' sponsor.

The last shirt brings us full circle and is the 2024/25 season Umbro yellow shirt worn by Jamie when playing in the B team. It is predominantly yellow with a simple round-neck collar. The yellow of the body is subtly broken up with tilted squares, each square filled with slightly different tints of orange. The Umbro badge is embroidered in black on the left of the shirt and the woven Hearts badge is on the right. This Umbro team shirt was also worn by West Ham United, Ipswich Town and Bournemouth.

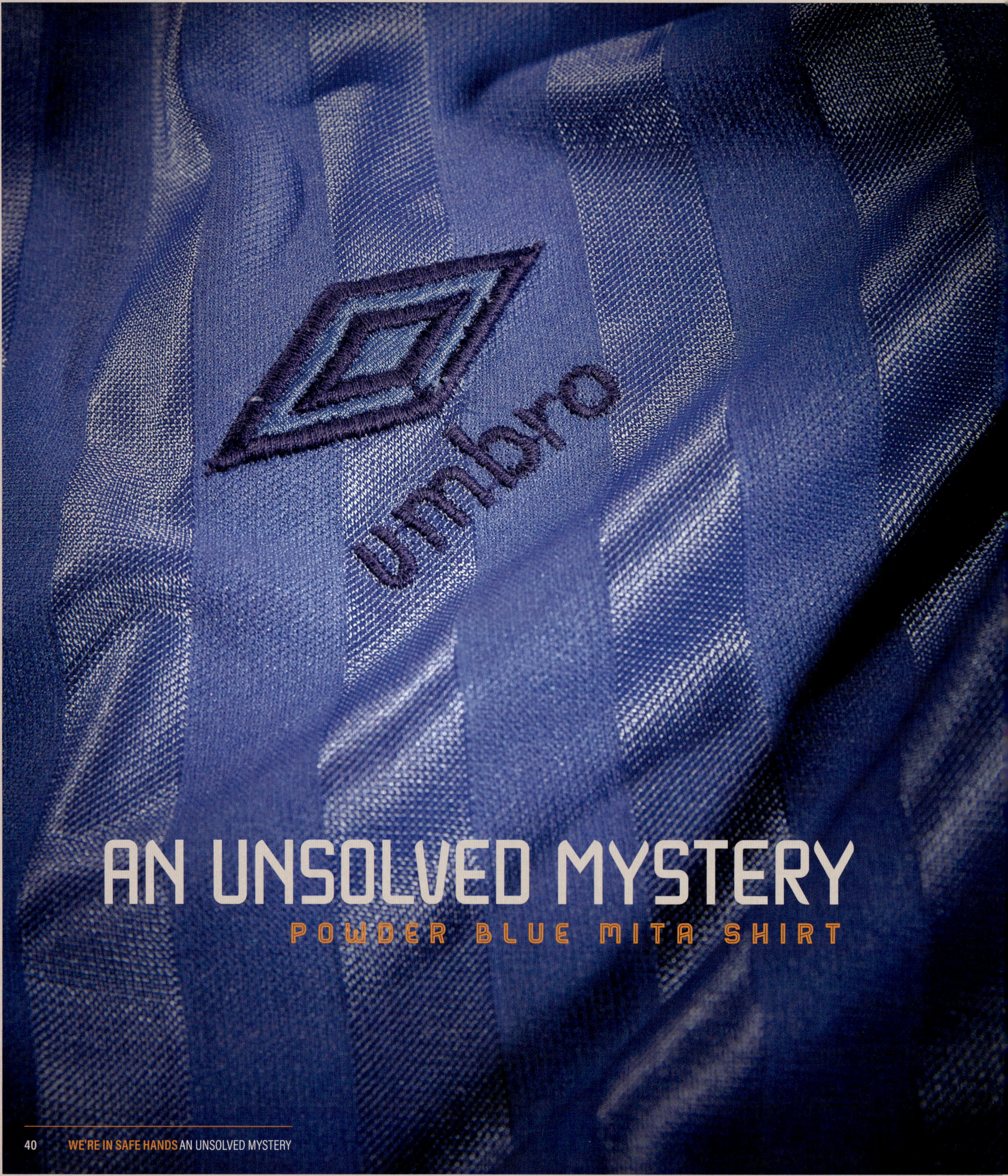

AN UNSOLVED MYSTERY

POWDER BLUE MITA SHIRT

1985/86

Hearts favourite Henry Smith has donned shirts from numerous manufacturers in countless designs throughout his illustrious career. Hearts fans, when asked to describe a shirt immediately associated with him, would likely give a variety of answers. These could range from the traditional black and yellow Umbro shirts of the early 80s to the brighter, bolder designs from Admiral and Asics in the late 80s and early 90s.

Almost certainly a shirt that wouldn't make it onto anyone's list is the rarely seen powder blue shirt from 1985/86. Throughout that season, Henry sported the classic Umbro yellow-bodied, black-sleeved, collared shirt. The powder blue variant appears in the traditional team photo taken at the start of the campaign, modelled by backup keeper Mark Cairns, but was rarely spotted thereafter. As far as I know, the shirt only made two and a half appearances in 1985/86. It was worn during both away matches against Motherwell in the league, and then for half a game at Tynecastle against Clydebank on 26 April 1986.

Eagle-eyed goalkeeping enthusiast Dougie Rankine noticed that Henry wore the yellow and black shirt for the first half, even though Clydebank had on their bright yellow away kit at Tynecastle that day. Referee Kevin O'Donnell of Airdrie must have missed the colour clash at kick-off but rectified his mistake at half-time, resulting in the 45-minute appearance.

The shirt then remained elusive for the rest of that season. However, it unexpectedly resurfaced two seasons later at Love Street in Paisley during a match against St Mirren! By 1987/88, Hearts had transitioned from Umbro to Bukta. Despite the change of manufacturer, the club was still associated with Mita, but the 1987/88 shirt was now emblazoned with Mita Copiers rather than just Mita.

THE UMBRO SHIRT WAS PART OF FORMER HEARTS KEEPER MARK CAIRNS' PERSONAL COLLECTION, GIVEN TO HIM BY HENRY. IT WAS AN UMBRO TEMPLATE, APPEARING IN THE MANUFACTURER'S 1985/86 CATALOGUE.

One question remains: how did Henry end up wearing an Umbro shirt that day? I posed it to him, hoping he might recall the details, but unfortunately, his memory didn't serve him well. Perhaps someone out there holds the key to this mystery. It would be fascinating to uncover the truth. Interestingly that day, the shirt turned out to be a stroke of luck for Henry. He kept a clean sheet, and Hearts secured a resounding victory, scoring six goals against the Buddies. John Colquhoun's hat-trick, along with two goals from John Robertson and one from Wayne Foster, contributed to the memorable outcome.

The Umbro shirt was part of former Hearts keeper Mark Cairns' personal collection, given to him by Henry. It was an Umbro template, appearing in the manufacturer's 1985/86 catalogue. Listed as 'Grobbelaar goalkeeper sweaters', it's described as diagonal shadow-striped with contrasting collar trim, shoulder and elbow padding, complete with a number on the back. At the time clubs had a choice of blue and two other colours: purple and green. Unsurprisingly, Hearts chose the blue shirt. It's a unique jersey and a great item to have in my collection.

2022/23 – 2023/24

FROM A DEBUT TO INTERNATIONAL RECOGNITION

ZANDER CLARK

Christmas Eve 2022 marked Zander Clark's competitive debut for Hearts under the most challenging of circumstances against Dundee United at Tannadice. In the 75th minute, Craig Gordon was involved in a horrific clash with United striker Steven Fletcher. Fletcher had chased a long ball from Australian keeper Mark Birighitti into the Hearts box, but Gordon reached it first, after which Fletcher collided with him.

Match referee Colin Steven initially awarded a penalty, but after a lengthy VAR check, he reversed his decision. Craig was in visible pain and was stretchered off the field wearing a leg brace. Zander came on with the game finely poised at 2-1 to United. Four minutes into injury time, goal machine Lawrence Shankland was brought down in the box, and a penalty was awarded. Shankland composed himself and slotted the ball past the diving Birighitti. It was later revealed that Craig had suffered a double leg break, meaning Zander would step in as Hearts' number one.

Zander had arrived at Tynecastle as a free agent after his contract with St Johnstone ended. He had earned legendary status at the Saints during the 2020/21 season when he was part of the team that secured the cup double, winning both the Scottish Cup and League Cup. Zander joined Hearts on a three-year contract after spending 11 years with St Johnstone. During that period, he had loan spells with Elgin City and Queen of the South.

Since taking over from club legend Craig Gordon, Zander has been in sparkling form. His performances earned him a spot in Steve Clarke's pool of players for the UEFA European Championship qualifiers. Having kept eight clean sheets in 15 games, his efforts did not go unnoticed at the international level, marking his first involvement with the Scotland squad since June 2021. Although he didn't start in Scotland's opening Group A match against Cyprus at Hampden on 25 March 2023, he became a regular on the bench for all subsequent games.

SCOTLAND
EST 1873
DECATHLON ARENA, LILLE
17 OCTOBER 2023
21

SCOTLAND
1873

THE 6FT 3IN STOPPER WAS HANDED HIS FIRST CAP IN THE SECOND HALF OF A HEAVY 4-1 FRIENDLY DEFEAT TO A STAR-STUDDED FRENCH TEAM, WHICH INCLUDED LIVERPOOL'S IBRAHIMA KONATÉ, ATLÉTICO MADRID'S ANTOINE GRIEZMANN, AC MILAN'S OLIVIER GIROUD AND PARIS SAINT-GERMAIN'S KYLIAN MBAPPÉ.

Fast forward to Tuesday, 17 October 2023, when Scotland played a friendly against France in Lille. The 6ft 3in stopper was handed his first cap in the second half of a heavy 4-1 friendly defeat to a star-studded French team, which included Liverpool's Ibrahima Konaté, Atlético Madrid's Antoine Griezmann, AC Milan's Olivier Giroud and Paris Saint-Germain's Kylian Mbappé.

Despite the loss, it was still a 'special occasion' for Clark, who also expressed his delight for fellow debutant Liam Kelly after the Motherwell captain's first-half appearance.

He told the Scottish press after the game, 'As a kid, you always dream of that moment. It was a great feeling, a proud moment. I'm buzzing for [Kelly] as well. I've known him since we were kids, so for both of us to get our first caps on the same night was special.'

Kelly echoed Zander's thoughts, adding, 'I've played for Scotland in every age group and been in a lot of squads beside big Zander, so I'm delighted to get that moment eventually and so grateful to the manager for giving me that chance. I'm delighted for big Zander because we've been in this together from the start.'

Surprisingly for a keeper of Zander's quality, he did not represent Scotland at any age-group level and was only called up to the senior squad at the age of 29. He said, 'Usually, you find that a lot of people who come through have been in the setup from a young age. To get into the senior squad with your first-ever call-up was a proud moment. Every time you get that email to say you have been selected, it's a very proud moment.'

Hearts gaffer Steven Naismith was delighted that Zander had been given his deserved opportunity, telling the local press, 'In his interview after the game, you can see how proud he was. From being on the fringes to making your Scotland debut is a massive thing. It is credit to him and Liam Kelly, for that matter, because both have been in a lot of squads and, if you like, have done their apprenticeship. They turn up, they are on call when needed and they are team players.'

Quite rightly, Zander was selected for Euro 2024. He spent his time on the bench as Steve Clarke preferred Norwich's Angus Gunn. Nonetheless, he follows in the footsteps of Hearts legend Henry Smith, who was in the Scotland squad for Euro 92 in Sweden.

At the time of writing, Zander has added three more caps to his collection, starting against Georgia and Norway in the Euro qualifiers in November 2023 and a friendly against Gibraltar in June 2024.

The four caps he has earned so far are a testament to his continuing outstanding form for Hearts. Having a club legend in Craig Gordon as his team-mate and rival for the number one spot can only be great for Zander and for Hearts. He has already pulled off some memorable saves early on in his career at Tynecastle.

His penalty save against Hibs on 27 December 2023 is one of my favourite stops. It meant Hearts would win 1-0 under pulsating circumstances. Early in the game, Lawrence

THE FOUR CAPS HE HAS EARNED SO FAR ARE A TESTAMENT TO HIS CONTINUING OUTSTANDING FORM FOR HEARTS.

Shankland had uncharacteristically missed a penalty. Before that miss, he was an amazing 15 from 15. With the game finely poised at 0-0, Hearts defender Kye Rowles did Clark's job for him in saving Dylan Vente's effort, and inevitably referee John Beaton pointed to the spot again. The goalkeeper had to be on his toes as Martin Boyle stepped up to the spot, sprawling to tremendously tip the Hibs talisman's effort onto the upright. Hibs would regret not taking advantage. Just as it looked as though the game was destined for a derby deadlock, skipper Shankland atoned for his penalty miss by curling the ball into the far corner to spark scenes of jubilation in the away end on 95 minutes. It also meant a tenth clean sheet of the

umbro
UEFA
FOUNDATION
for children

umbro
GB USA ASIA EUR
L L XL L

'PENALTIES CAN GO ANYWHERE REALLY, BUT WE ALWAYS DO LOOK OVER THEM. YOU CAN'T REALLY SAY THEY WILL GO THIS WAY OR ANOTHER; IT'S HOW YOU FEEL IN THE MOMENT.'

season for Zander and a very merry Christmas and a happy new year for the Hearts fans.

After the game, Zander was asked about the penalty save. He told the local papers, 'Penalties can go anywhere really, but we always do look over them. You can't really say they will go this way or another; it's how you feel in the moment. But I was probably due one, and it got our fans going again and gave everyone a lift. We'd had the chance to go one up and missed the penalty, so it was a horrible feeling when we then conceded a penalty. I knew that if we lost a goal, the mood would have been flatter, but it's those sorts of moments you know you can go and give the team a lift if you save it. It was brilliant. Listen, it wasn't a classic, and we knew it was going to take a bit of magic to turn the game, but when you have Shanks up there, he's more than capable of producing it – and what a finish it was. I think it was more relief getting the three points when it looked like it was only going to be one, and it obviously creates a bit of distance from them at the minute.'

This standout moment is the one which won him the Most Memorable Moment trophy at Hearts' end-of-season awards night. Recounting the 2023/24 campaign and his saves, Zander said, 'There have been a few, but probably the Hibs penalty save in terms of how the game went up until that point. To keep the scores level, and then for Shanks to notch right at the death, I'd probably say that was the highlight.'

Another moment that stands out as a stunner was Zander's save against Kilmarnock at Tynecastle on 30 March 2023. It was made in stoppage time of the first half when he produced a save out of the top drawer to claw away a Marley Watkins header that seemed destined for the net. The stop made sure of the 1-1 draw.

Lastly, his save against Tom Lawrence of Rangers in the 2024/25 season opener at Tynecastle was as good as I've seen. The Welshman unleashed a 22-yard volley destined for the top corner, but Clark sprung high to his left for a right-handed touch over the crossbar, helping secure a 0-0 draw.

I have featured my personal favourites from my shirt collection which Zander has worn or are his match-prepared shirt for a game.

The first is his match-prepared Scotland shirt from his debut against France in Lille. It was manufactured by adidas. This shirt is primarily green with subtle patterning to add texture to the body. Its long sleeves are also green to the elbows and feature the famous three adidas stripes in white; the rest of the sleeve to the cuff is black. The vinyl adidas logo is on the left of the chest, with a woven Scotland national team badge on the right. The Sporting ID name set is solid white, and the number is in a perforated style on the back of the shirt. Zander wore number 21 on the night. His match shirt also had the sleeves cut from the elbow in the exact same way as he does for his club shirts. In a recent interview I asked Zander why he did this. He explained that when training he would always wear a T-shirt and on occasion a base layer, so felt he wanted to replicate that during a game.

The next two Umbro shirts are from Hearts' UEFA Europa Conference League campaign of 2022/23. Zander was on the bench for all six of Hearts' games, both home and away, against Latvian side FK RFS, Italian giants Fiorentina, and from Turkey, İstanbul Başakşehir.

One is a bench-worn away shirt featuring the MND Scotland sponsor; the club shop version had Stellar Omada as the sponsor. The bright orange Umbro shirt has a patterned effect across the shoulders which follows all the way down to the cuffs of the sleeve. Zander's preference is short sleeves which Umbro did not produce, and therefore the kitman chopped

WE WILL REMEMBER THEM
F H
1874

cinch
PREMIERSHIP

the sleeves off for him. The shirt also has the UEFA Foundation sleeve badges on the left and Stellar Omada sponsor on the right sleeve. Sporting ID provided the Euro name set and numbers for the back of the shirt, which were solid white. Zander's squad number was 28. It was worn against Fiorentina and İstanbul Başakşehir at home.

The other European shirt is the predominantly yellow top which has a black band that runs from the shoulder to the bottom of the shirt and has matching black cuffs, although again Zander chose to have the sleeves chopped. It's also notable that the players' version of this shirt is different from the club shop version as it doesn't have an embroidered badge; it has a heat-pressed woven badge. The Sporting ID name set and number are in a classy solid maroon. Worn on the night with yellow shorts and yellow socks, it had a brilliant retro feel about it. It was worn against Riga home and away as well as Fiorentina and İstanbul Başakşehir away.

The last shirt is the Umbro away version from season 2023/24. It's from the home game against Livingston at Tynecastle on 1 November 2023, Hearts winning 1-0 thanks to a Kenneth Vargas goal. Former Hearts keeper Jack Hamilton was in goal for Livvy, and it was thanks to him that the Men in Maroon only scored one goal. The

ZANDER WAS ON THE BENCH FOR ALL SIX OF HEARTS' UEFA EUROPA CONFERENCE LEAGUE MATCHES OF 2022/23, BOTH HOME AND AWAY.

shirt that day featured the poppy and the words 'We Will Remember Them'. It's now a club tradition to feature the embroidered poppy to commemorate Remembrance Sunday and to honour servicemen and women who have lost their lives in all conflicts since the First World War. The shirt is simple and unfussy in blue. It has a solid luminous band very close to the elbow of the sleeve. Just like the Euro shirts, the sleeves have been cut. It has a heat press vinyl Cinch Premiership sleeve badge on the left-hand side. MND Scotland was the club sponsor. The back of the shirt has official SPL oversized player-issue letters and numbers made by Sporting ID.

Zander kindly agreed to spend some time with me and have a chat about all things football, including the shirt collection that he has amassed over his playing career.

I asked about the people who have had the biggest influence on his career, and without hesitation, the reply was his mum and dad, who, like many other parents, ferried their child to training sessions and games from an early age and attended so many games without giving it a thought. His dad influenced Zander's decision about taking his place between the sticks as he had been a goalkeeper in the local works team.

The stopper also listed the keepers that he most admired, with Gianluigi Buffon, Manuel Neuer, Iker Casillas and René Higuita all getting a mention. One player slightly from left field was former Spanish international Santiago Cañizares, who played for Valencia and Real Madrid and retired at the age of 39 after making exactly 500 club league appearances in senior football. Zander liked the overall style of Cañizares with his trademark crop of dyed blond hair and his meticulous matching kit. He would always try and have matching boots and shirts, a trend that a younger Zander would also always try to follow.

We inevitably got on to the subject of shirts, and I asked if Zander kept hold of or swapped shirts. It then transpired that he is quite the shirt connoisseur. He tends to swap with players that he has played

H·M
C
F
1874

with or if the opportunity arises in Europe or on trips with Scotland, he swaps with opposition players. His collection contains some impressive keepers from at home and abroad. On home soil, he has swapped with the likes of Allan McGregor, Fraser Forster and Joe Hart. Trips with St Johnstone and Hearts abroad have seen the big stopper bring home swaps from some great players. This includes Galatasaray skipper Fernando Muslera, who was Zander's opposite number when St Johnstone lined up against the Turkish giants in August 2021. Clark almost missed out on the shirt after Muslera was red-carded on 55 minutes after blatantly pulling down Chris Kane in the box and conceding a penalty. Muslera disappeared up the tunnel and wasn't seen again. Zander asked the Galatasaray kitman if the keeper had left his match shirt, but the answer was no. He did manage to swap with former Atlético Madrid and Barcelona midfielder Arda Turan. Fast forward to the second leg in Perth, a pulsating match which saw the Turkish side win 4-2 and St Johnstone exit Europe. After the game, Zander heard a low whistle directed at him, so he turned around, and it was the Galatasaray kitman who handed over Muslera's shirt from the first leg. A kind gesture from his opposite number who didn't make the trip to Scotland due to his suspension.

I also asked Zander if he had a favourite kit that he had worn. He had a fondness for a full pink number that was worn in 2018/19 with St Johnstone. Maybe Hearts will produce a similar kit in years to come.

He also had a special mention for Bristol City and the goalkeeper shirts that they had produced over the last few seasons, particularly the Hummel efforts. Definitely a man who keeps his eye on shirts!

A TEENAGE SENSATION

IAN WESTWATER

1981/82

Ian Westwater was born in Loughborough, England, but moved to Edinburgh when he was a boy. As a promising youth player at the all-conquering Salvesen Boys Club in Edinburgh, he played alongside Davie Bowman, Gary Mackay, John Robertson and Stuart Gauld. He was making a name for himself at that level and was contacted by the English FA to play for England Schoolboys but opted to play for Scotland. Several senior clubs were chasing Ian for his signature, but he chose Hearts, believing he might have a better chance to play for the first team. Ian had taken advice from his dad on the move. He was always destined to be a goalkeeper as his dad had also been a professional goalkeeper for Queen of the South and Arbroath.

At the tender age of just 16 years, 11 months and 24 days, Westwater became the youngest goalkeeper to play a first-team game for Hearts. He still holds the record as the youngest ever keeper to play in the Scottish Premier League. He made his competitive debut for the club on 1 November 1980, in front of a crowd of 5,707 at Tynecastle against St Mirren. The game ended 1-1 with Alfie Conn Jr. scoring the equaliser for Hearts in the 76th minute.

When I spoke to Ian about making his debut, he told me he wasn't quite as nervous as he possibly should have been as he had played in the East of Scotland Shield Final against Hibs on 20 August 1980 at Tynecastle in front of a crowd of just over 7,000. The line-up that day was littered with first-team players like Jim Jefferies, Stuart Gauld, Crawford Boyd and Willie Gibson. His ex-Salvesen team-mates Dave Bowman

and Gary Mackay also started. The game ended 2-2 and eventually went to a penalty shoot-out with Hearts losing 5-4. A great experience for Ian.

His debut came on the back of a series of bad results for Hearts. Manager Bobby Moncur was vocal in the press about giving youth a chance. The week before, Bobby had watched Westwater, Mackay and Bowman play a key role in the Scotland Youth team at Ayr. With little to no money to bring in new players, he was convinced that playing the young starlets was the way forward for the club. He was quoted in the local papers as saying, 'There are lots of youngsters coming through in the reserves. The three who were at Ayr are only some of them. We've been very active signing youngsters, and I see this as the only way for a club like ours to succeed. I feel sure the supporters would rather their stars were home-produced.' Bobby was true to his word with all three youngsters making their debuts for the club during the 1980/81 season, all before their 17th birthday. Bowman played 23 games, Mackay 15 and understandably for a keeper, Ian played twice during the season.

Ian received positive reviews after his first game against St Mirren. Ian Wood of *The Scotsman* wrote, 'As first appearances go, this one worked out well for him, with his early tests being reasonable shots from comfortably long range with which he dealt competently. Thus encouraged, he went on to give a sound all-round display which could have done his confidence no harm at all.'

Ian made his second and final appearance of the season against Dundee United at Tynecastle. The Terrors' line-up included the likes of Frank Kopel, Paul Hegarty, David Narey and Paul Sturrock. United ran out easy 3-0 winners against a struggling Hearts team.

Moncur restored the more experienced John Brough to the starting 11 for the next game against Morton and the big keeper kept his place for the remainder of the season.

It didn't stop Ian working extremely hard in training, working alongside John Brough and Thomson Allan. Ian remembers both keepers sharing great tips for matchdays. One he got from Allan always stuck; during the game Allan would follow the ball everywhere in the stadium, helping him keep his focus for the entire 90 minutes. A tip that Ian would use during his career.

Ian's Hearts career was hindered by a career-threatening injury to his right knee, sustained while playing for a Scotland under-17 and under-18 team against Brazil in a 1981 youth tournament in Cannes. He was out of the game for nine months. He recovered and was part of the squad that won the 1982 UEFA European Under-18 Championship in Finland. It is still the only tournament that Scotland has won at any level.

With the signing of Henry Smith at the beginning of the 1981/82 season, Ian and John played only bit-part roles for the rest of their time at the club. Westwater left having played four competitive matches and kept one clean sheet. Ian then signed for Dunfermline in July 1984 and went on to have an extremely successful career with the Pars. In two spells for the Fife club, he made 361 appearances and kept 115 clean sheets. He also helped Dunfermline achieve promotion to the Scottish Premier League in the 1995/96 season.

The featured shirt was thought to belong to Ian but that's not conclusive. It was also thought to have been worn by him in a pre-season game but through the mists of time these details have been lost. It sports the unusual number 18 and is believed to be from the 1981/82 season. The shirt has an interesting history after it was worn. It, along with four other outfield shirts, was given to the original vendor for a newly created five-a-side team that members of Edinburgh-based Tanfield Bowling Club were playing in. Tanfield member Stan Barclay, the managing director of Alexanders, who would sponsor Hearts during the 1983/84 and 1984/85 seasons, managed to pull a few strings to provide

a full set for the team. The shirts were surplus to requirement as Hearts transitioned to a bold new style of shirt, with Alexanders sponsoring the front of the famous maroon shirts. A good friend who knew that I was writing a book all about Hearts goalkeepers asked if I would like to add this rare shirt to my collection and without hesitation I said yes.

This keeper shirt is a timeless classic. Manufactured by Umbro, it features the iconic black double diamond tape on the sleeves, a definitive football strip design flourish of the 1970s. Hearts had worn this design since 1977. The shirt is undoubtedly from 1979/80 onwards. This fact can be verified due to the embroidered wordmark appearing below the logo in lower-case lettering. The shirt boasts a winged collar and a vivid yellow body with a large, embroidered club badge on the right-hand side. The number on the back is white stitched cloth, numbered 18. An absolute classic. It's a very rare shirt as, to my knowledge, very few have survived.

THE GREATEST HONOUR

SCOTLAND SHIRTS

1991/92 – 2024/25

Not including Celtic and Rangers, Hearts have produced the most senior Scotland internationals with a grand total of 88 players at the time of writing. Among them are eight goalkeepers.

Craig Gordon has won 50 caps while playing for Hearts. His first came at the age of 21 years and five months against Trinidad and Tobago at Easter Road on 30 May 2004, with Scotland winning 4-1. Amazingly, Craig's Scotland career spans 20 years: on 7 June 2024, he made his 75th and what appeared to be his final appearance in a 2-2 draw with Finland at Hampden. To all intents and purposes Craig had bowed out of the international scene. The Finland game was Scotland's final outing before they made the trip to Germany for the European Championship. Steve Clarke had inexplicably omitted Craig from the squad, instead opting for Angus Gunn, Liam Kelly and Hearts' very own Zander Clark. Fast forward four months, or 122 days, and Craig was back, recalled for the Nations League fixtures against Croatia and Portugal.

Explaining his decision, Clarke said, 'He's the number one at Hearts and he's playing every week. Zander has been on the bench; Liam Kelly is on the bench at Rangers and Robby McCrorie is on the bench at Kilmarnock. I need three goalkeepers so what better than to bring Craig back?

'Craig told me it [the Finland game] was not a farewell and that he'd see me in the future. So, he's lived up to his promise. It's absolutely a testament to him; he's always shown that he's up for the fight. He wants to play every week and as many times as he can for his country. I'm looking forward to seeing him again.

V
ESTADIO ALGARVE, FARO
3 JUNE 2024
SCOTLAND
EST
1873
21

JIM CRUICKSHANK EARNED NINE CAPS OVER A PERIOD OF 11 YEARS AND SEVEN MONTHS. HE MADE HIS DEBUT AT 23 YEARS OLD AGAINST WEST GERMANY AT THE NIEDERSACHSENSTADION IN HANOVER, IN FRONT OF A MASSIVE CROWD OF 65,000.

'He shows durability. He's a good professional, and like I said before, somebody who just wants to prolong his playing career as long as he can. Hats off to Craig.'

Craig featured in both fixtures and, following further Nations League matches against Portugal, Croatia and Poland, he hoisted his cap tally to 79 and counting. He kept consecutive clean sheets in the Nations League in October and November 2024 as Scotland drew 0-0 with Portugal and beat Croatia 1-0. This was followed by a 2-1 win over Poland on 18 November, which saw Gordon become the third-oldest player to compete in European competition at 41 years and 322 days. On 20 March 2025, Gordon made his 80th Scotland appearance against Greece in the Nations League 2025 play-off, joining Kenny Dalglish, Jim Leighton, Darren Fletcher and Andrew Robertson as the only players to hit the 80-cap mark. He then played the return leg against Greece and hit cap number 81. Quite a remarkable story.

Jim Cruickshank earned nine caps over a period of 11 years and seven months. He made his debut at 23 years old against West Germany at the Niedersachsenstadion in Hanover, in front of a massive crowd of 65,000. The game ended in a 2-2 draw. His last appearance was against Romania on 17 December 1975 in a Euro 76 qualifier at Hampden, a 1-1 draw.

UMBRO
EURO 92
SWEDEN
12

THE SCOTTISH FOOTBALL
ASSOCIATION
EURO 92
SWEDEN

HENRY SMITH HAD THREE CAPS, AGAINST SAUDI ARABIA, NORTHERN IRELAND AND CANADA, AND DIDN'T LOSE A GAME WHEN HE WAS IN BETWEEN THE STICKS FOR SCOTLAND.

Jack Harkness played for Scotland 12 times, achieving three caps while playing for Queen's Park and nine while at Hearts. He is best remembered for being part of the 'Wembley Wizards', the Scotland team that famously defeated England 5-1 at Wembley on 31 March 1928. This match is legendary in Scottish football history due to the unexpected and emphatic victory over their rivals on English soil. The team earned the nickname because of their dazzling performance, showcasing skilful and stylish play. Standout players from that match included Alex Jackson of Huddersfield Town, who scored a hat-trick, and the legendary Arsenal inside right Alex James.

Again at the time of writing, Zander Clark has earned four caps during his time at Tynecastle. Henry Smith had three caps, against Saudi Arabia, Northern Ireland and Canada, and didn't lose a game when he was in between the sticks for Scotland. Harry Rennie also won two caps.

One of Harry's appearances came in a 4-1 win against England at Celtic Park on 7 April 1900. The crowd of 63,000 set a new world record attendance for an official international match. On the day, Scotland wore a shirt featuring Lord Rosebery's racing colours of pink and primrose. In later years, these

ON 28 MARCH 2025, CRAIG GORDON BECOME THE THIRD-OLDEST PLAYER TO COMPETE IN EUROPEAN COMPETITION FOR SCOTLAND AT 41 YEARS AND 322 DAYS, JOINING KENNY DALGLISH, JIM LEIGHTON, DARREN FLETCHER AND ANDREW ROBERTSON AS THE ONLY PLAYERS TO HIT THE 80-CAP MARK.

colours gained notoriety when Hearts produced an away kit in 2016/17 that paid tribute to Lord Rosebery. That version was very much marmite at the time but is now very coveted by collectors. It is also worth noting that Harry was renowned as a goalkeeping innovator. He introduced several game-changing concepts to goalkeeping in Scottish football. He was the first to demark his goal area to assist him with judging angles, while he also pioneered the study of opposing forwards' gestures and body language as they prepared to shoot. His scientific approach quickly brought him to national prominence, and he signed for Hearts from Morton in 1898 for £50.

Nicky Walker earned a solitary cap, and Willie Waugh did the same. Willie was one of the best keepers the club has ever had. Signed in 1928, he was unlucky to be the understudy to Jack Harkness. An interesting fact is that in 1936, he was loaned out to Hibs to help save them from relegation, a plan which succeeded. Upon returning to Tynecastle at the end of the season, he became the first-choice

SCOTLAND

SCOTLAND
Official licensed product
DIADORA

OVER THE YEARS, SCOTLAND SHIRTS HAVE BEEN CRAFTED BY RENOWNED MANUFACTURERS SUCH AS UMBRO, DIADORA, FILA AND ADIDAS. EACH OF THESE BRANDS HAVE PRODUCED ICONIC DESIGNS, PARTICULARLY FOR GOALKEEPER SHIRTS.

keeper and retained that spot until the war. His solitary cap came against Czechoslovakia in a friendly at Ibrox Stadium, where Scotland strolled to a 5-0 victory. Willie was accompanied by three of his Tynecastle team-mates that day: Andy Anderson, Andy Black and Tommy Walker.

Over the years, Scotland shirts have been crafted by renowned manufacturers such as Umbro, Diadora, Fila and adidas. Each of these brands have produced iconic designs, particularly for goalkeeper shirts. I am fortunate to own several memorable shirts worn by former and current Hearts goalkeepers, spanning various age levels from under-17s to full internationals. Some of these shirts are instantly recognisable, while others may be less familiar.

The Euro 92 shirts, designed by Umbro and featured in the book, are the home and the alternative versions. Both were prepared for Henry Smith for the tournament. The alternative shirt is a striking turquoise green, accented with a black collar and cuffs. The centre showcases a series of black triangles arranged in a V-shape, trimmed with

THE EURO 92 SHIRTS, DESIGNED BY UMBRO, ARE THE HOME AND THE ALTERNATIVE VERSIONS. BOTH WERE PREPARED FOR HENRY SMITH FOR THE TOURNAMENT.

dark red. This design debuted at the 1991 FA Cup Final worn by Nottingham Forest's Mark Crossley, where Tottenham Hotspur triumphed 2-1. By autumn, the template was adopted by several teams with Umbro contracts including Celtic, Everton and Tottenham, who received bespoke styles. Other teams such as Aston Villa, Chelsea, Ipswich Town, Leeds, Manchester City and Newcastle United also sported this template. Variations in green, yellow and purple were common, and a blue version was notably worn by Andy Rhodes of Dunfermline.

The home shirt, predominantly black with purple and green flashes, was worn by Andy Goram in all three of Scotland's Group B games. There was an away kit with the same design, but the predominant colours were yellow and grey.

In October 2006, Craig Gordon wore the Diadora gold home shirt against France in their Euro 2008 qualifier. He was joined by team-mates Steven Pressley and Paul Hartley. Scotland triumphed 1-0 thanks to a goal from Gary Caldwell. This shirt is a

THE SCOTTISH FOOTBALL
ASSOCIATION
EURO 92
SWEDEN

THE HOME SHIRT, PREDOMINANTLY BLACK WITH PURPLE AND GREEN FLASHES, WAS WORN BY ANDY GORAM IN ALL THREE OF SCOTLAND'S GROUP B GAMES. THERE WAS AN AWAY KIT WITH THE SAME DESIGN, BUT THE PREDOMINANT COLOURS WERE YELLOW AND GREY.

match-prepared version, given to the original vendor after the game. It also appeared in a couple of the pre-game promotional shots. The match-worn version features short sleeves, cut at the elbows by the kitman. That season Scotland had two home versions, with Craig also wearing the red version during the qualifiers.

Fast forward to the present and we have Zander Clark's bench-worn shirt from the 2024/25 UEFA Nations League group stage game against Portugal in Lisbon, where Scotland lost 2-1. This away shirt features a bold purple colourway with contrasting green graphics, finished with the iconic adidas branding on the chest and the Scotland team crest. Bright and bold indeed! I purchased this shirt for my collection as it was worn on my son Luke's 13th birthday.

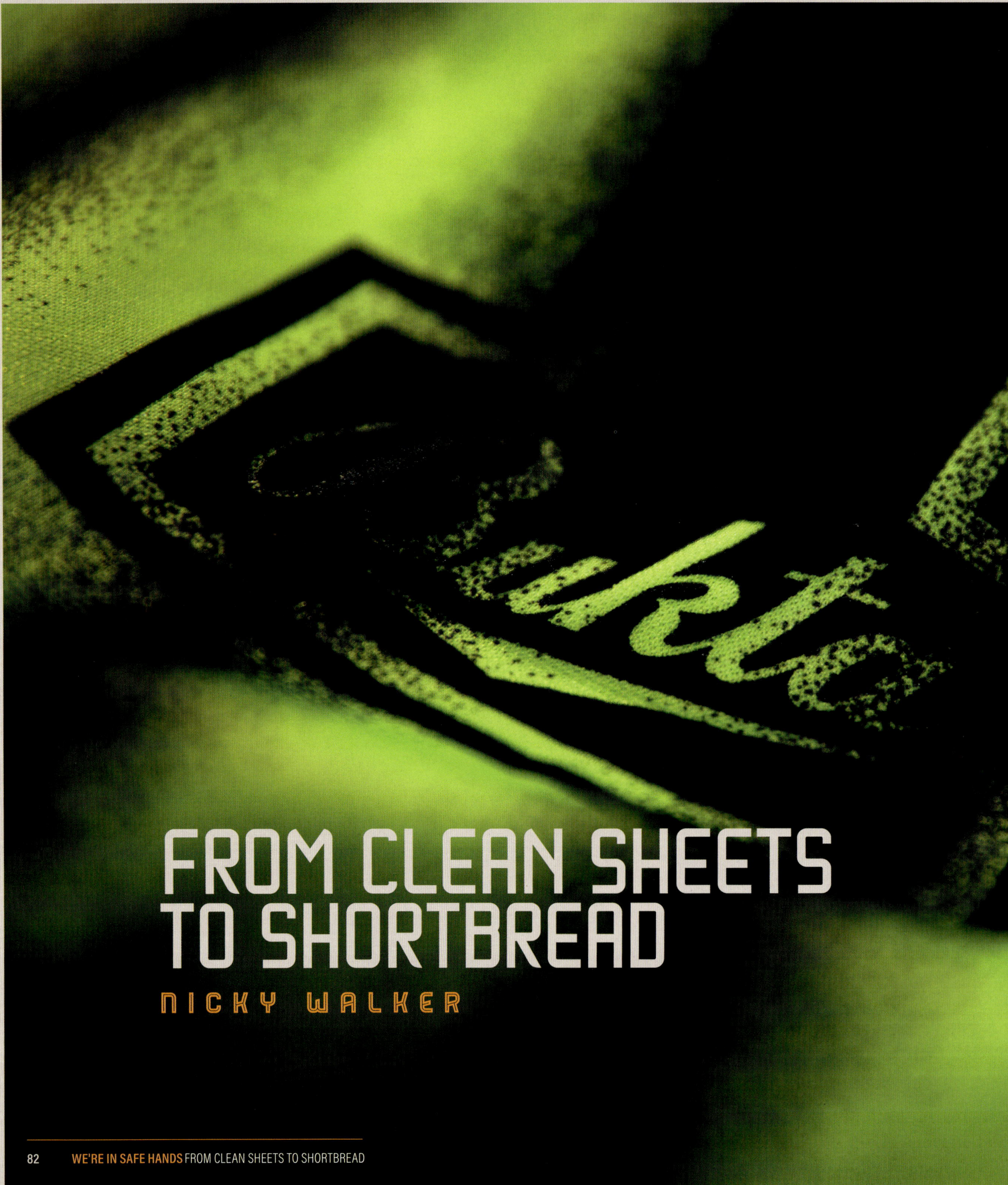

FROM CLEAN SHEETS TO SHORTBREAD

NICKY WALKER

1990/91

Bought by Alex MacDonald for £125,000 in July 1989 from Rangers, Nicky Walker joined Hearts alongside other summer signings which included the experienced David McCreery from Newcastle United, and striker Husref Musemić from Red Star Belgrade. Nicky made his debut on 26 September 1989 against Manchester United at Tynecastle in front of 9,001 fans for Eamonn Bannon's testimonial. Hearts lost the game 4-2; Nicky came on at half-time for Henry Smith. The Manchester United team included stars like Jim Leighton, Viv Anderson, Gary Pallister, Brian McClair and Mark Hughes.

Nicky had to be patient to get a game in the first team and it wasn't until the 1990/91 season under new manager Joe Jordan that he made his competitive debut. This came against Dundee United at Tynecastle in a 2-1 win on 16 February 1991. It was a winning start for Walker, and after the game Jordan praised him, saying, 'Nicky was playing in his first Premier Division match for two years because of the consistency of Henry Smith. He did everything that was asked of him and was desperately unlucky when United scored, as he had made a magnificent save from John Clark earlier.'

Joe decided to play Nicky after Hearts suffered a heavy 5-0 defeat at Pittodrie against Aberdeen. He appeared to lose faith in Henry Smith, who had strung together almost 200 consecutive appearances, and played Nicky for the remainder of the season. The 1991/92 season saw Henry return between the sticks. Hearts finished a superb second in the league with Henry playing 53 games, only equalled by Dave McPherson.

Heart of Midlothian F.C.
H M F C
1874
GARY MACKAY
TESTIMONIAL 1990-91

Bukta

ON 24 MARCH 1993, NICKY'S FORM SAW HIM EARN HIS SOLITARY CAP FOR SCOTLAND, JOINING HEARTS TEAM-MATES CRAIG LEVEIN, ALAN MCLAREN AND JOHN ROBERTSON IN THE STARTING LINE-UP AGAINST GERMANY.

Nicky's competitive battle with Henry for the number one slot continued, and in 1992/93 he played 22 games to Smith's 32. However, in 1993/94, it was 34 to 17 in Henry's favour. On 24 March 1993, Nicky's form saw him earn his solitary cap for Scotland, joining his Hearts team-mates Craig Levein, Alan McLaren and John Robertson in the starting line-up against Germany. Scotland lost 1-0 thanks to a Karl-Heinz Riedle goal in front of 36,500 fans at Ibrox Stadium.

Nicky's time at Hearts came to an end after making a total of 50 league appearances for the club. His last game was against St Johnstone on 31 August 1994. By then the manager was Tommy McLean, who did not seem keen on either Nicky or Henry. Nicky was swapped for Scotland B international Craig Nelson with the Jags receiving £100,000. Wayne Foster also joined Nicky at Partick Thistle, and they remain great friends to this day.

I was lucky enough to catch up with Nicky and asked him to reflect on his time in Gorgie. He immediately mentioned his Easter Road derby debut during Hearts' impressive 22-game unbeaten run against Hibs between 1989 and 1993. The pressure on the players to maintain the ongoing streak was immense. He felt a profound sense of relief when he and his team-mates left Leith with a clean sheet, satisfied with his performance. The *Evening News* captured the moment perfectly with the headline 'In good Nick' recognising his outstanding performance.

The stopper made a string of spectacular saves as Hibs launched a whirlwind start. Within four minutes, Walker dived bravely at the feet of Keith Wright and Mickey Weir and made a full-length dive to stop a deflected shot from Darren Jackson. Near the end of the game, Walker pulled off another incredible save from a Tommy McIntyre header. It's certainly a game that will always stand out for him.

But Nicky also acknowledged the tough times. He mentioned a game that still irks him: the third round of the Scottish League Cup against St Johnstone at Tynecastle. Hearts were leading 2-0 thanks to goals from Gary Locke and John Colquhoun. However, a mistake by Nicky in the 38th minute led to Stevie Frail being red-carded for handling the ball on the line. Although Walker saved the penalty and the deflected rebound, Hearts went into the break 2-0 up with a one-man deficit. St Johnstone seized the initiative in the second half and eventually won 4-2. It was Nicky's last game for the club, a tough memory to recall.

Amid the challenges, Nicky fondly remembers his call-up for Scotland against Germany at Ibrox. Although they lost 1-0, and he joked that Craig Levein's back pass led to the goal, he beamed with pride knowing his family had attended the match.

Nicky held a special appreciation for Henry Smith, praising both their training camaraderie and Smith's character. Henry was the first to congratulate Nicky on his Scotland call. When Nicky joined Hearts, he believed it spurred Henry to greater heights and an outstanding level of consistency that meant Nicky had to wait a year to make his competitive debut.

He also cherished working with other great goalkeepers at Hearts like Gary O'Connor and Mark Cairns, who made his time at the club enjoyable. Nicky hoped he had played a small part in nurturing the careers of younger players like Allan Johnston, Gary Locke, Paul Ritchie and Alan McManus. He looks back on his time at Hearts as a special period in his career.

Nicky played for Hearts when arguably goalkeeper shirts were at their most flamboyant, with both Bukta and Admiral producing some eye-catching tops.

I have featured a shirt which hopefully encapsulates the Bukta era. It was worn by Nicky in Gary Mackay's testimonial against Everton on 13 May 1991. Bukta is a historic sportswear brand that was founded in 1879 by Edward R. Buck and Sons in Stockport, England. Originally known as E.R. Buck and Sons, the company initially produced shorts for soldiers fighting in the Boer Wars. Bukta quickly expanded into producing football and rugby equipment, becoming one of the longest-established football kit apparel manufacturers in the United Kingdom.

This shirt was a template and was also worn by Dundee United, Newcastle United and Bristol City in the 1991/92 season. It features a black button-down collar and cuffs. Black runs the length of the shoulders, breaking just before the elbows, and continues as a thick band around the sleeves at the elbows. The body of the shirt is luminous yellow with a vertical faded-effect thick pinstripe running through it. The distinctive Bukta logo sits on the left of the shirt, with the Hearts crest on the right. It's a unique and well-thought-out design. The back of the shirt showcases the iconic felt Bukta number in black.

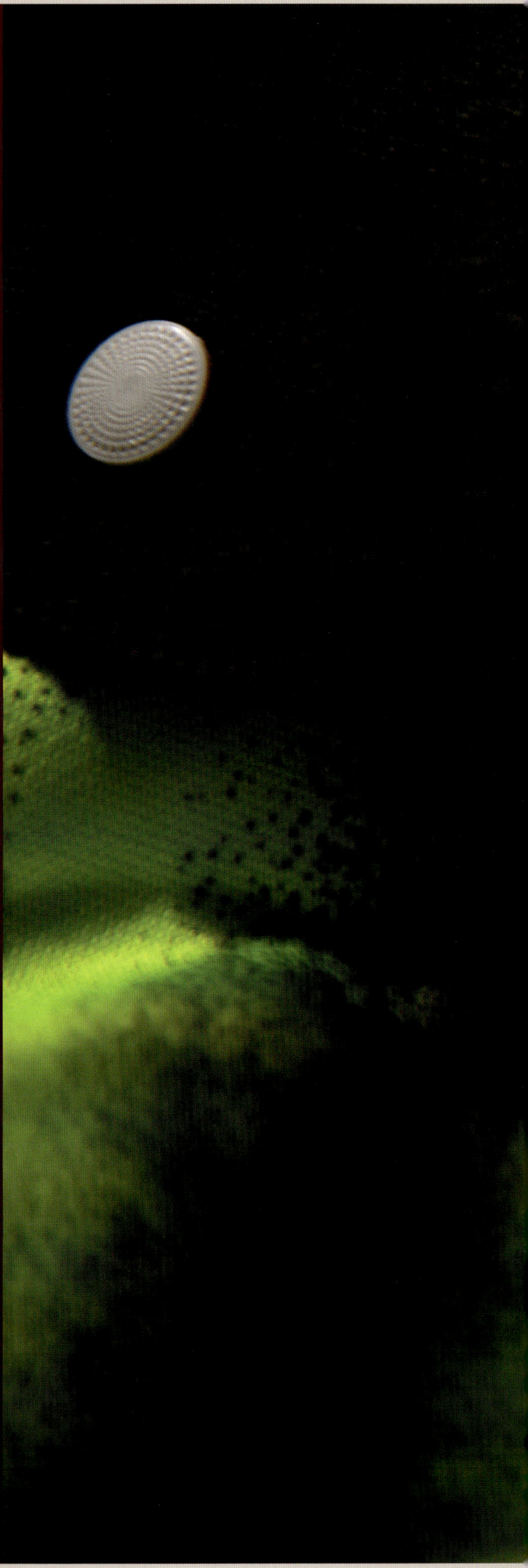

THIS SHIRT WAS WORN BY NICKY IN GARY MACKAY'S TESTIMONIAL AGAINST EVERTON ON 13 MAY 1991.

HMFC
1874
HENRY SMITH
TESTIMONIAL
V EVERTON
2nd AUGUST 1993

1993/94

THE SHIRT THAT NEVER WAS

HENRY SMITH TESTIMONIAL

On Monday, 2 August 1993, Hearts welcomed Everton to Tynecastle for goalkeeping legend Henry Smith's testimonial. A crowd of 9,213 visited the stadium to pay homage to the popular stopper. Everton showed 'H' the greatest respect when they arrived in Edinburgh with a team that included household names such as Neville Southall, Dave Watson, Paul Rideout, Mo Johnston, Peter Beagrie and Tony Cottee. The Hearts fans who attended were delighted to get their first glimpse of new signings Justin Fashanu and Peter van de Ven in Gorgie. The Toffees won 2-0 thanks to goals from Cottee and Matt Jackson.

In previous seasons, most testimonial matches featured either a new shirt or a different sponsor as well as embroidery on the shirt to commemorate the occasion. In the 1992/93 season, John Robertson played against Newcastle United in a one-off white shirt with Fastech as the sponsor with embroidery around the badge. In 1990/91, Gary Mackay played against Everton in the Bukta home shirt that had embroidery commemorating the game and Lothian Plumbing Supplies as the

asics

sponsor. Bucking the trend was Eamonn Bannon's testimonial against Manchester United in 1989/90. The team wore their Bukta home kit sponsored by Thorn Security. Jump back to 1987/88 for Walter Kidd's testimonial against Everton. The team wore that season's Bukta home shirt with Mita Copiers as the usual sponsor, but the shirt was embroidered with the match details.

It seemed a given that Henry Smith would have a shirt, likely the home top, with embroidered match details of the game. However, on the day that wasn't the case. The players sported the away Inter Milan-style shirt, which was worn during the regular league campaign. Over the years shirts have appeared on the market with embroidery underneath the Hearts crest with the wording 'Henry Smith Testimonial v Everton 2nd August 1993'. The testimonial committee likely planned to produce a special kit but decided not to proceed with the idea. I was fortunate enough to acquire a version of the goalkeeper shirt with the testimonial detailing. Perhaps this was a sample presented to Henry and the testimonial committee but was rejected. Henry went on to wear the players' version of this shirt during the game.

The shirt was made by Asics and was a template. It is an absolute fan favourite. After attending a club event and getting the chance to chat about keepers' shirts with Craig Gordon, he mentioned to me that this shirt is among his favourites produced by the club. It was the away shirt for the season and made a few appearances. It encapsulates the brightly coloured shirts that emerged in the early 90s with its visually striking rainbow-coloured abstract squares design, making it stand out from the crowd. It was also worn by English teams such as Newcastle United, Aston Villa and Blackburn Rovers.

A match-worn version of this shirt is almost impossible to track down with the replica version also proving exceedingly difficult to obtain. If any Hearts fan does have this shirt, they are extremely lucky!

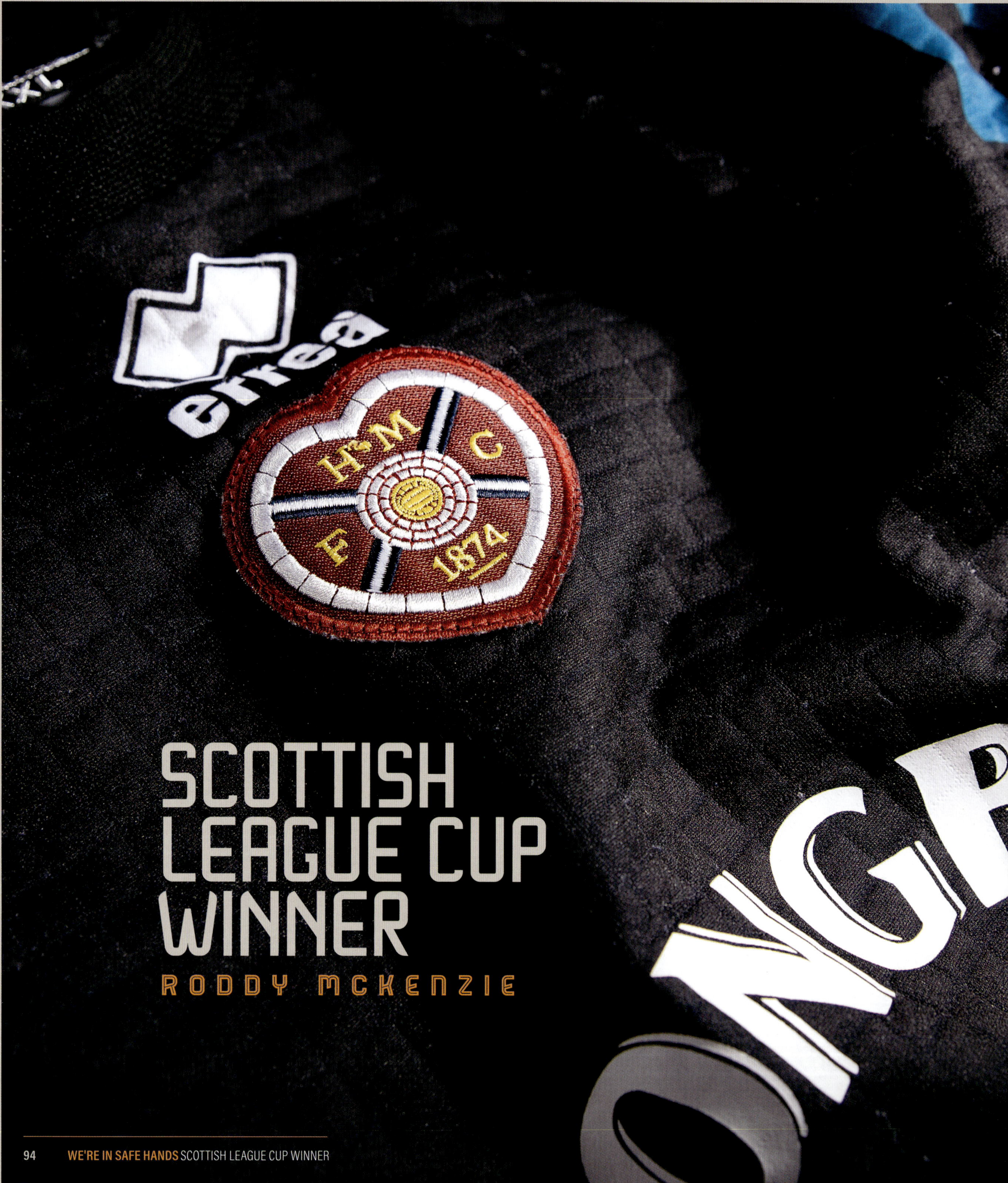

SCOTTISH LEAGUE CUP WINNER

RODDY MCKENZIE

2001/02

Hearts' opening game of the 1993/94 season was against Rangers at Ibrox. It was a memorable day for goalkeeper Roddy McKenzie, who was just a month shy of his 18th birthday, and took his place on the bench for the first time alongside Ian Ferguson and Allan Johnston. However, like many young keepers, it took a while before he made his competitive debut. This came during the 1996/97 season under manager Jim Jefferies, away to Aberdeen on 10 February 1997. In the meantime, Roddy gained valuable experience during a year-long loan at Stenhousemuir in 1995/96.

During his time with the Warriors, Roddy played a crucial role in their victory in the Scottish Challenge Cup Final, saving a penalty in the 5-4 shoot-out win against Dundee United after a goalless draw following extra time.

Back to the game at Pittodrie. With Gilles Rousset sustaining an injury in the previous match against Kilmarnock, Jefferies gave McKenzie the nod. He didn't disappoint in the 0-0 draw. Roddy produced a mature performance on a night marked by driving wind and rain throughout the 90 minutes. Notably for shirt collectors, Hearts wore the rarely seen yellow and black Pony away kit. McKenzie made two more appearances in 1996/97, playing in the last two games against Dundee United and Rangers.

It's fair to say that Roddy wasn't the luckiest player at Hearts. After biding his time as an understudy to Gilles Rousset and then Antti Niemi, he was given the opportunity to potentially cement his place as the number one keeper when Antti departed for Southampton in August 2002. Craig Levein placed his faith in Roddy and put a young Craig Gordon on the bench.

However, disaster struck for Roddy after an extended run in the team; he broke his finger while at Hearts' training camp in Portugal during the winter break. It was a huge blow for Roddy, and Craig Gordon deputised for him in the Scottish Cup game against Falkirk. Manager Craig Levein signed Finn Tepi Moilanen, who went on to play in goal for the remainder of the season. At the time, Levein told the press how he felt about the goalkeeping situation just before signing Tepi, saying, 'It's tough on Roddy as he has waited a long time to get his chance and hasn't let anyone down when he's played. He has had to try and live up to the previous keepers such as Henry Smith, Gilles Rousset and Antti Niemi. He is not an Antti Niemi – who is – but in his own way, he has probably done as well if not better than I expected.'

Roddy left Hearts at the end of the season having played 54 competitive games and kept 16 clean sheets.

It certainly wasn't the end of Roddy's career, in fact, he went on to add to his Stenhousemuir Challenge Cup winners' medal with a Scottish League Cup winners' medal while playing for Livingston. He helped the club win their first major honour when

BANK OF SCOTLAND
SPL

THIS SHIRT WAS PRODUCED BY ERREA, BASED IN PARMA, ITALY, AND WAS WORN BY RODDY IN ONE OF HIS SIX GAMES IN THE 2001/02 SEASON.

they defeated Hibernian 2-0 in the 2004 final. Roddy became a stalwart with Livi, making 100 appearances during his three and a half year stint. He moved to Dunfermline in 2006 but was plagued by injury. Eventually, he returned to Livingston at the beginning of the 2008/09 season, making a further 56 appearances.

It's a credit to Roddy that he had a great career and tasted success. He is always mentioned by his peers at Hearts as a top keeper and equally a top person.

This shirt was produced by Erreà, based in Parma, Italy, and was worn by Roddy in one of his six games in the 2001/02 season. Erreà has manufactured kits for some of Europe's top football clubs. This stylish blue and black number features a black round-neck collar and cuffs. The centre of the body is black, with the sleeves and periphery of the body in blue, interspersed with a black pattern design and sporting the Bank of Scotland vinyl sleeve badges. The sponsor, Strongbow, is prominently displayed. The Erreà logo sits just under the centre of the collar, with the Hearts crest positioned below it. Sporting ID numbers and name set adorn the back of the shirt. McKenzie wore number 13.

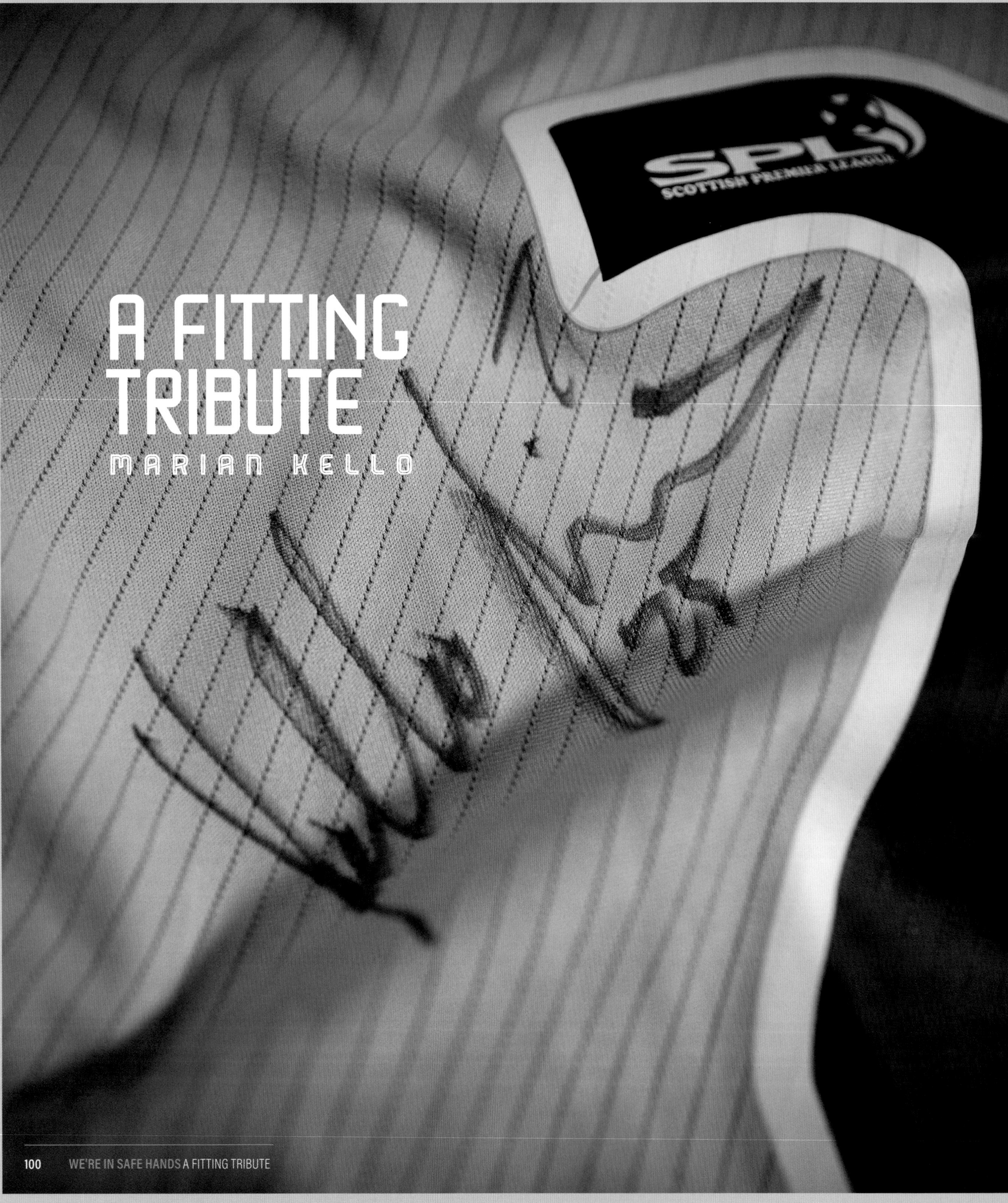

A FITTING TRIBUTE

MARIAN KELLO

2008/09

A game that will be fondly remembered by Hearts fans is the 2-0 home victory against Hamilton on 20 November 2010. It was the day that the supporters and goalkeeper Marián Kello paid tribute to the late, great Jim Cruickshank. This match marked Hearts' fourth consecutive 2-0 triumph, keeping them firmly in third in the SPL, riding high after a sixth win in their last seven matches. Kello kept a clean sheet in each of those successes with the Men in Maroon scoring an impressive 12 goals. During that sequence of wins, they recorded victories over Hibs and Celtic, and Rudi Skácel notched a hat-trick against St Mirren. But when the dust settled, it was a tale of two Jims.

Tynecastle was awash with emotion following a minute's silence to honour the memory of the legendary Jim Cruickshank, who had passed away the previous week at the age of 69. The chatter in the local pubs before and after the game was all about Cruicky, with fans reminiscing on his outstanding performances over the years.

In a fitting tribute, the current guardian of the Tynecastle goal, Marián Kello, tied a yellow goalie's jersey to his net. Marián produced a man-of-the-match performance which was crowned when he mirrored Cruickshank's penalty-saving skills with a spectacular save, thwarting Simon Mensing's attempt to claw Hamilton back into the game. Jim would surely have been looking down on the hallowed turf and nodding in appreciation.

The other Jim, manager Jefferies, couldn't have asked for a better way to honour his former team-mate from the 1970s. He told the *Evening News*, 'Jim was a great penalty saver. Isn't it fitting that Marián comes out with the trademark yellow shirt and makes a phenomenal penalty save on the day we pay our respects to him?'

Kello's save ensured that Hearts, despite not reaching the dizzying heights of some of their recent performances, also gave Jefferies a perfect gift ahead of his 60th birthday. The boss had made it clear before the game that all he wanted as a present was another three points, and his players delivered.

Just after the half-hour mark, Skácel broke the deadlock with a daring opener. The Czech midfielder capitalised on a throw-in that Martin Canning had allowed to bounce, sending a stunning, dipping shot with that wand of a left foot over a desperate dive from Tomáš Černý from 30 yards out on the left side of the box.

'We were a bit slow off the mark, but then we looked for that spark of quality and Skácel provided it,' Jefferies acknowledged.

KELLO'S SAVE ENSURED THAT HEARTS, DESPITE NOT REACHING THE DIZZYING HEIGHTS OF SOME OF THEIR RECENT PERFORMANCES, GAVE JEFFERIES A PERFECT GIFT AHEAD OF HIS 60TH BIRTHDAY.

OFFICIAL UMBRO TEAM PRODUCT

Not to be outdone, wing wizard David 'Temps' Templeton tried to outshine Skácel with an equally spectacular strike barely six minutes into the second half. Templeton curled a fantastic shot from distance into the roof of the net from well outside the area.

During the game the footballing gods shone on Kello, who may not have been as familiar with the remarkable service Cruickshank gave Hearts as those supporters who fell silent for a minute before kick-off, but that didn't stop him from drawing inspiration from the Tynecastle legend and Hall of Fame inductee. 'It was an emotional afternoon for me,' Kello admitted to the *Evening News*. 'I was a bit agitated at times during the game, but it was just because of the situation. I felt a connection with Jim, and I really wanted to keep a clean sheet for him.' The Slovakian certainly did Jim and the Hearts support proud.

Kello had already produced an incredible performance that the man himself would have been proud of.

'I WAS A BIT AGITATED AT TIMES DURING THE GAME, BUT IT WAS JUST BECAUSE OF THE SITUATION. I FELT A CONNECTION WITH JIM, AND I REALLY WANTED TO KEEP A CLEAN SHEET FOR HIM.'

The month before, Marián had produced a string of saves in a narrow 2-1 defeat to Rangers in the league. It included fingertip saves from Vladimír Weiss and Steven Davis and then a block with his legs in what looked sure to be a second goal for Kyle Lafferty from close range. The stop from Davis, which he somehow managed to push onto his right-hand post and out for a corner, would win the SPL's Save of the Season award for 2010/11. Marián would go on to pick up three prizes at the club's end-of-season awards night, being named player of the year, supporters' player of the year, and taking the trophy for the save of the season. Quite a haul. Kello's form at Hearts would see him get three caps for Slovakia including games against Luxembourg and Andorra.

In early April 2012, Kello agreed an early release from the club with his contract due to expire in the summer. He had not played since refusing a January transfer to Austria Vienna. On his departure he told the BBC, 'I would like to take this opportunity to thank my team-mates and the Hearts supporters who have always made me feel so welcome. I will always value my time at the club and wish them all the very best for the rest of the season.'

Kello would play 86 competitive games for Hearts, keeping 32 clean sheets and saving four of the nine penalties he faced, including the one against Hamiton.

This powder blue Umbro shirt from 2008/09 has a diagonal shadow stripe on the body with a contrasting grey collar, shoulder, and cuff trim. The large club badge is woven and on the right side of the shirt, with the black Umbro 'double diamond' logo on the left. The shirt also features the black heat-pressed vinyl sponsor, Ukio Bankas, in the centre. The back of the shirt has the official Sporting ID Scottish SPFL white numbers and name set as well as a small Scottish saltire underneath the collar. Kello's squad number was 25 throughout his time with the club.

2014/15

Neil Alexander was the first-choice keeper at Hearts during the 2014/15 and 2015/16 seasons. He made 32 appearances in his first campaign, which would have been more had he not been injured in the opener against Rangers at Ibrox. The following season he made 40 appearances with only Sam Nicholson making more on an impressive 43. Prince Buaben equalled Neil, also playing 40 times.

LIVING THE DREAM

NEIL ALEXANDER

SPFL

During those two seasons, Neil managed 31 clean sheets and averaged a one-goal-per-game concession rate. I think it's fair to say that when Hearts signed Neil , there was an air of surprise around the move. The club had decided to release first-choice keeper Jamie MacDonald as well as his backup Mark Ridgers, leaving a real need to bring in an experienced number one.

They decided that Neil was the man they wanted between the sticks. The former Rangers and Scotland player joined as player-coach on 1 July 2014, when his contract expired with Crystal Palace. He was looking forward to playing regular first-team football again after only featuring once for the Eagles in the League Cup.

Neil told the *Edinburgh Evening News*, 'I am delighted to get the chance to join a club I have supported for many years. With the coaching side of it as well, this is a fantastic opportunity for me.' Adding a little more context, he went on to explain, 'At 36, I need to start looking to the future and want to get involved in coaching. The club has given me a great chance to get a foot on the ladder.'

Incidentally, Neil would not be the only recruit from Crystal Palace in 2014/15. Osman Sow was someone Neil knew well from his time in London. He teamed up with Sow when the big Swedish striker featured as a trialist in a friendly against East Fife at Bayview. Sow netted the third goal in the 3-0 win. Afterwards, Neil said, 'Big Oz was injured for the first part of the season. But I played alongside him in training, under-21 and reserve games. He has loads of ability and lots of enthusiasm.' Both Alexander and Osman would turn out to be inspired signings.

If Neil joining Hearts was somewhat unexpected it would be remiss of me not to mention his exit from Tynecastle. The Edinburgh-born stopper had been offered a new contract after helping them secure a third-place finish in the league and with that, European football for the following season. It was suddenly withdrawn and Neil then headed north to Aberdeen. Manager Robbie Neilson was comfortable with his decision, telling *The Scotsman*, 'I must make the decisions that are best for the football club. Neil is still a very good goalkeeper and will do very well, but I had to decide for the club. I felt it was the best decision to give Jack [Hamilton] the opportunity to be our number one and bring Paul Gallacher in as our goalkeeper coach. Jack needs that and I felt it was the right time for him.'

When researching for the book I managed to catch up with Neil, who at the time of writing was the goalkeeper coach at Motherwell. He looked back at his time at Hearts with fondness and some regret. Neil is a boyhood Hearts fan who loved watching his heroes John Robertson and Henry Smith. His parents bought him a new Hearts shirt every season, which was normally an outfield shirt. Interestingly, he played in central midfield for his school team, but goalkeeping was always his first love. He had admired the skills of two legendary keepers when growing up: Andy Goram for his sheer ability to move around the area with ease and Peter Schmeichel for his bravery, leadership and organisational skills. When the chance came along to sign for the team he supported as a boy, he jumped at it. He felt that his two seasons at Hearts were the best of his career, performing to an extremely high standard on the pitch and enjoying the mentor role to a young Hearts squad. Neil would have loved to have had the opportunity to hit 100 appearances for Hearts as well as experience a European night under the lights at Tynecastle, but alas, it wasn't to be.

He recalled some of the highlights of his time at the club. Neil chuckled when talking about the 10-0 win against Cowdenbeath on 28 February 2015. He was quite a spectator for most of the game, but the gallows humour of the Hearts crowd came into play when he was announced as the man of the match at the final whistle. Neil found this highly amusing and enjoyed his trip to the Gorgie Suite to pick up his bottle of champagne.

Neil also enjoyed a bird's eye view of the famous equalising goal scored by Alim Öztürk at Easter Road in the dying minutes of the League game on the 26th of October 2014. The win extended Hearts unbeaten start to the league campaign. What he remembered most was running the length of the pitch to celebrate with his team-mates. He also admitted that, like the

HEART OF MID-LOTHIAN F.C. LTD.
1914-1915

adidas
FORMOTION

THE YELLOW SHIRT WAS ONLY WORN WHEN HEARTS WORE THEIR TIMELESS ARGENTINA-STYLE AWAY SHIRT WHICH ALSO FEATURED THE FOUNDATION OF HEARTS LOGO.

rest of the Hearts support, he had thought at the time, 'Don't shoot from there.'

Another game in which Neil remembers celebrating wildly is the 2-2 draw against Celtic on 27 December 2015 at Tynecastle. It wasn't so much the draw Neil was celebrating; it was the fact that Osman Sow smashed in a 25-yard equaliser in the dying seconds of stoppage time. When the ball flew into the net Neil sprinted from his goal past the Wheatfield Stand, high-fiving fans as he ran towards his jubilant team-mates. Happy times.

We got on to the subject of shirts. When I asked him what his favourite top was from his career, without hesitation, he said the adidas white shirt that he wore when playing for Hearts in 2014/15.

This shirt has a simple white round-neck collar. It was part of the adidas Onore 14 2014/15 range, designed especially for goalkeepers and was used at the 2014 World Cup. Player-worn shirts would have a heat-pressed club badge on the right and a woven black adidas logo on the left-hand side. The famous three stripes in black run from the neck to the white cuff. The white body is broken up with an orange curved vertical panel which runs down again from the neck to the bottom of the shirt on both sides, gradually changing from a bright orange to a more muted orange at the hem. As with the other shirts that season, it has a vinyl heat-pressed SPFL logo on both sleeves. The shirt features a unique badge for the 2014/15 season which was seen as a fitting tribute to the team of 1914/15. This

shirt features the poppy in the centre and was worn by Neil against Raith Rovers on 8 November 2014.

The range came in several colours including yellow, orange, green and white. Many teams wore the template in 2014/15 with clubs such as Sunderland and West Ham United wearing yellow. National teams including Germany and Spain wore varying colours of green. Scotland wore a light green and a red version of the shirt.

Neil went on to say that he loved the shirt so much that he had a hand in the choice of colours for the Hearts keepers' kits for the 2017/18 season, which would be produced by Puma. Yes, you've guessed it, he chose a white shirt. Ironically, he wouldn't get to wear it. Jack Hamilton did and again it was a real beauty.

He also mentioned a superstition that he had around the shirts he wore. Whenever possible, he would not change his shirt if the team were on a winning streak.

Neil had some outstanding games and saves during his two seasons with the club, but did a particular save stand out for him? His two saves against Dundee United at Tannadice from striker Edward Ofere, both from headers and both from very close range, were his favourites. He added that he had made a few against Hibs which he felt were up there, and a stop at Hamilton which he managed to claw out was also one he was proud of.

The second shirt featured is also from 2014/15 and it's an adidas yellow and black number. It features an unfussy black round neck collar with a white trim. The body is a vivid yellow and has the woven black adidas logo on the left-hand side with a woven Hearts badge on the right. The famous three stripes in white run from the neck to the shoulders. There is then a space leaving room for the SPFL sleeve badges. The stripes then continue to the black cuffs. In the centre is the Foundation of Hearts logo. This shirt was only worn when Hearts wore their timeless Argentina-style away shirt which also featured the Foundation of Hearts logo. A classic shirt from a classic season.

1997/98
OLYMPIC
SPORTSWEA

THE ROSEBURN BAR SHIRT

GILLES ROUSSET

Most UK football fans might not be familiar with the shirt manufacturer Olympic Sportswear. Hearts most famously wore a shirt produced by them when they won the Scottish Cup in May 1998. So, which other clubs or nations wore Olympic? Between 1998 and 2001, they provided shirts for several teams including Portugal, who wore an Olympic kit during Euro 96. This makes sense given that they are a Portuguese company. Interestingly, they spent some time trying to break into the Belgian market in the mid-1990s with limited success. They then turned their attention to the lucrative British market.

Olympic managed to sign contracts with clubs like Dundee United, Rushden & Diamonds, Scarborough, Luton Town and Southend United. They also managed to get Northern Ireland on board. They seemed to be making progress, but it came to a sudden halt in the 2000/01 season when their association with Luton ended, as did their presence in the UK. Hearts had already ended their link with Olympic at the end of the 1999/2000 season and opted for Erreà in 2000/01.

BETWEEN 1998 AND 2001, OLYMPIC PROVIDED SHIRTS FOR SEVERAL TEAMS INCLUDING PORTUGAL, WHO WORE THE BRAND DURING EURO 96.

The most popular template shirt that Olympic produced was seen around Scottish and English grounds in 1997/98 and was worn by Gilles Rousset frequently throughout that season. It is a yellow, black and orange tiled effect shirt with a large black round-neck collar, matching sleeves and cuffs. The Olympic Sportswear logo is prominently displayed across the high round-neck collar in white. This shirt was most famously worn by Gilles in the 1998 Scottish Cup Final. It is also the only keeper shirt in the official team photograph for 1997/98.

This brings me to my mystery shirt produced by Olympic Sportswear. It is correctly badged with SPFL sleeve badges and has the unusual number 16 in black. It has a predominantly grey body, a popular colour for Hearts' keeper shirts over the last few decades. Like the shirt described above, it also has a large black round-neck collar, matching sleeves and cuffs. There is grey padding at the elbows with the same grey on the body of the shirt on the front and back. The Olympic Sportswear logo is again displayed across the high round neck collar in white. It appears to be from

S·F·L

1874

I KNOW FOR CERTAIN THAT THIS SHIRT IS NOT THE ONLY ONE OF ITS KIND IN EXISTENCE AS I HAVE SEEN ANOTHER. IT'S IN A FRAME IN THE ROSEBURN BAR NEAR TYNECASTLE, WHICH HAS BEEN A PUB SINCE THE 1880S.

1997/98 but tracking down photographic evidence of it being used in a game has been difficult. In fact, I can't find any at all!

I know for certain that it is not the only shirt of its kind in existence as I have seen another. It's in a frame in the Roseburn Bar near Tynecastle. The Roseburn Bar has been a pub since the 1880s. A lot of the original fixtures remain. It consists of the public bar, the lounge and the jug bar or fly half. The public bar is split into three sections by partitions, called trap one, trap two and trap three. Each trap is like a different pub with many customers sticking to certain areas, which can lead to some healthy rivalry. Many moons ago, women were only allowed in the jug bar from where they were served through a hatch and there was no female toilet. Today, the Roseburn is a busy pub with a great atmosphere and is popular with locals, as well as football and rugby fans heading for Tynecastle or Murrayfield stadium on matchdays. But back to the shirt: it is signed beautifully front and centre by Scottish Cup-winning goalkeeper Gilles Rousset. The detailing on the shirt is identical to the one I have in my collection. I often wonder if it has the number 1 on the back of the shirt.

Gilles did wear a grey and black shirt when Hearts visited Motherwell on 4 October, which can be viewed on YouTube, but it's not the shirt I have. On further scrutiny, the Olympic Sportswear logo doesn't appear to be present. He then wears a version which resembles the home kit but has more of a multicoloured almost Aztec pattern on the body, which appears to be the favoured away shirt. A few different versions were worn on the club's travels around SPFL opposition, but no sign of mine. Perhaps it was only ever worn in a reserve game or was a template that was rejected by the club? It's an oddity in the collection, that's for sure. Maybe someone out there spotted it on their travels. If you did, get in touch.

Heart of Midlothian F.C.
H M
F C
1874

1988/89

A VIENNESE WALTZ

MARK CAIRNS

A young Mark Cairns was with Hearts during the 1987/88 and 1988/89 seasons. Unfortunately, he didn't manage to register a competitive appearance, although he was involved in some memorable moments. One notable instance was when he was on the bench for Hearts' famous 1-0 UEFA Cup second round away victory against Austria Vienna on 9 November 1988, thanks to a solitary goal from Mike Galloway.

Cairns also enjoyed loan spells at Berwick Rangers and East Stirlingshire during his time with Hearts. After his stint at Tynecastle, his football journey took him to various other Scottish clubs including Gala Fairydean, Partick Thistle, Alloa Athletic, Brechin City, Queen's Park, Stirling Albion and Arbroath. He made over 200 senior appearances for these clubs.

Arguably, his biggest achievement in the game was the Scottish Challenge Cup triumph while playing for Alloa. Mark etched his name into the Wasps' history books for his endeavours during the 1999 final. It was a pulsating match against Inverness Caledonian Thistle

THIS SHIRT IS THE ONE THAT MARK WORE WHEN HE WAS ON THE BENCH AGAINST AUSTRIA VIENNA IN THE UEFA CUP IN 1988/89.

on 21 November at the Excelsior Stadium in Airdrie. This was Alloa's first national final in their 121-year history, while Inverness Caledonian Thistle had reached their first final since being founded in 1994. The tournament specifically featured clubs below the Scottish Premier League, with Inverness from the First Division and Alloa Athletic from the Second Division.

The match, played in front of 4000 fans, was a rollercoaster of goals and drama. Alloa led 2-1 at half-time but, shortly after the interval, both teams scored making it 3-2 by the 47th minute. Inverness equalised with a second penalty from Paul Sheerin in the 56th minute, resulting in a 3-3 scoreline after 90 minutes. The game went into extra time where Alloa's Martin Cameron scored his second goal to take a 4-3 lead. However, Sheerin completed his hat-trick for Inverness, levelling the score at 4-4 and forcing a penalty shoot-out. This would be Mark's time to shine.

As always, five players were nominated to take penalty kicks. Willie Irvine took the first for Alloa and scored. Sheerin took Inverness's first penalty and, despite scoring three goals during the game two of which were from 12 yards, he missed. David Beaton then struck the bar and missed for Alloa. Mark McCulloch levelled for Inverness at 2-2. Both teams

MARCA REG.

THIS SHIRT WAS GIVEN TO ME BY MARK, WHO SWAPPED IT WITH GOALKEEPER WELLINGTON TAVARES FAJARDO WHEN HIS BRAZILIAN CLUB, CRUZEIRO, VISITED EDINBURGH FOR A FRIENDLY MATCH AT TYNECASTLE.

then scored their next three penalties to make it 4-4 from five attempts each; it was now sudden death. Mark Cairns stepped up to take the penalty and scored. He then saved Teasdale's attempt to ensure Alloa won 5-4 in the shoot-out. It was a real *Roy of the Rovers* moment, a day to remember for the former Gracemount High pupil.

The first shirt featured is the one that Mark wore when he was on the bench against Austria Vienna in the UEFA Cup in 1988/89. It was made by Bukta, who had been supplying kits to Hearts since the 1986/87 season and would continue doing so until 1990/91. Interestingly for this game the shirt had no sponsor, the same being true for the previous round against St Patrick's Athletic and then for the next European tie against Velež Mostar. The Novafone logo would first appear on the shirts at the league home game against Rangers on 10 December and would then remain for the rest of the season.

The shirt has a grey body and features matching black collar and cuffs, as well as black patches running from the cuff to the elbows. Bukta sublimated their logo into the shirt, giving it a unique feel. The number also stands out with the word Bukta featuring vertically in the number itself.

THE CRUZEIRO OUTFIELD PLAYERS WORE BLUE ADIDAS SHIRTS FEATURING THEIR SPONSOR, COCA-COLA, ON BOTH THE FRONT AND BACK. INTERESTINGLY, THE GOALKEEPER'S SHIRT WAS NOT MADE BY ADIDAS BUT BY THE BRAZILIAN MANUFACTURER TRIERRI.

Player-worn shirts from the 1988/89 season would have both an embroidered club badge and Bukta logo on the front. The version made available to the fans via the shop was a heat-pressed flock logo and a heat-pressed plastic badge.

The next shirt in the book is unique as it's the only one that isn't a Heart of Midlothian top. This one was given to me by Mark, who swapped it with goalkeeper Wellington Tavares Fajardo when his Brazilian club, Cruzeiro, visited Edinburgh for a friendly match at Tynecastle. Although Mark was part of the squad, he didn't make it to the bench. Hearts emerged victorious with a 2-1 win thanks to a penalty by Kenny Black and an 88th-minute winner from Iain Ferguson, marking his home debut.

The Cruzeiro outfield players donned blue adidas shirts prominently featuring their sponsor, Coca-Cola, on both the front and back. Interestingly, the goalkeeper's shirt was not made by adidas but by the Brazilian manufacturer Trierri. It also displays the Coca-Cola logo on both sides. This discrepancy remains one of those intriguing shirt mysteries. Why wasn't the keeper wearing adidas? I wanted to include a South American shirt to compare it with a Scottish shirt from the late 80s. It's worth noting that Scottish clubs did not begin exploring additional sponsorship opportunities, including back-of-shirt and sleeve sponsorships, until the late 90s. This is a great and unique shirt to have in my collection.

adidas

HEART OF MIDLOTHIAN F.C.
1874
KICK OFF
2009
FULL TIME
2010
18
TYNECASTLE STADIUM
74
UMBRO
OFFICIAL FOOTBALL SHIRT

2009/10

HALF-TIME HERO

JANOS BALOGH

János Balogh joined Hearts on an initial six-month loan in August 2008 from Debreceni VSC. He was expected to be strong competition for Márian Kello and Jamie MacDonald for a place in the starting line-up. On 19 October 2008, he made an unexpected debut as a half-time replacement for the injured Kello in the Edinburgh derby at Easter Road. The match ended 1–1 with Balogh making a crucial save to deny Derek Riordan a winning goal in the dying minutes.

He signed for Hearts on a permanent deal on 2 February 2009 from Debreceni for a fee of £185,000. After spending the early part of his career battling Kello for a place in the first team, he eventually lost out to the Slovakian and spent much of his time on the bench. With the emergence of MacDonald he slipped to third choice, making only one appearance in the 2011/12 season. He left Hearts in December 2011 having made 41 appearances in all competitions.

One statistic that sticks out about Balogh is his penalty record. During his time with Hearts, he faced four penalties and was only beaten once. Not a bad return.

The first spot-kick he faced was from former Hearts hero Paul Hartley who was now wearing the green and white hoops of Celtic. Hartley had taken 17 penalties for Hearts and successfully converted them all. With

ŪKIO
BANKAS
SELLS

Celtic already 2-0 up at Tynecastle on 2 November 2008, Hearts were up against it. The likelihood of a comeback looked even bleaker when Marius Žaliūkas was shown a controversial red card after he was adjudged to have pulled Scott MacDonald's shirt inside the box. TV evidence would later prove that the foul had taken place outside. Regardless, Hartley stepped up and duly pulled the attempt past Balogh's right hand post, much to the delight of the Hearts support.

János would face his second penalty against Dundee United at Tannadice on 28 February 2009. Hearts won 1-0 in a game that was critical in the race for third place and would see János turn in a man-of-the-match performance against the Terrors. Notably, he prevented United going ahead early in the game with a double save from Fran Sandaza and Paul Caddis on 13 minutes. His handling was outstanding throughout the game. Hearts went ahead on 62 minutes from a fine strike by Michael Stewart. With the game finally poised the referee pointed to the spot with ten minutes to go after Sandaza took a tumble in the box. The decision against Eggert Jónsson, in what looked like a precisely timed tackle, looked very harsh. Justice was served when Balogh saved to his right from a weak Sandaza effort. After the game, Stewart said, 'János came up trumps and managed to make sure we got three points.' On the penalty incident, he commented, 'I wasn't far away from the incident and my initial reaction is that it was a horrendous decision. Thankfully János saved it and we've managed to hang on for a massive result.'

Balogh would come up short against Rangers when Hearts lost 2-1 at home on 23 August 2008. He couldn't prevent a well-placed Kris Boyd conversion on 88 minutes after Ismaël Bouzid made contact with Steven Naismith in the box and referee Craig Thomson pointed to the spot.

ONE STATISTIC THAT STICKS OUT ABOUT BALOGH IS HIS PENALTY RECORD. DURING HIS TIME WITH HEARTS, HE FACED FOUR PENALTIES AND WAS ONLY BEATEN ONCE. NOT A BAD RETURN.

The fourth and final penalty János would face would be in an away game against Kilmarnock on 28 November 2009. With Csaba László's Hearts struggling at the wrong end of the table, 3 points were vital. Hearts delivered and steered themselves up the league. Two second half goals from Eggert Jónsson and Christian Nadé would see them secure a 2-1 win. Five minutes from time Balogh saved from a poorly struck penalty from the robust Kevin Kyle making it three from four for the Hungarian stopper.

After his time with Hearts, he returned to Hungary and continued his playing career with Nyíregyháza and Debreceni. At the time of writing, he was the goalkeeper coach with Debreceni.

This shirt is from the 2009/10 season. While the light blue Umbro shirt was frequently seen throughout the campaign, this black and gold version was also worn in several games, including the memorable 2-1 win against Hibs at Tynecastle on 20 March 2010. During the same season, English Premier League sides like West Ham United, Hull City and Sunderland also wore Umbro kits.

The Hearts shirt followed a similar template, with West Ham's keepers wearing a black and blue version, Hull in black and light blue and Sunderland in black and grey. The Hearts top features a large black panel across the shoulders and down to a quarter of the shirt's length, extending to the elbow of the sleeves. The remainder of the sleeves are gold with a small black patch from the wrist to the elbow. The rest of the body is a solid gold colour. It was a rather unusual choice of colour for the club.

The large club badge is woven and on the right side of the shirt, with the white Umbro double diamond logo on the left. The shirt also features the heat-pressed vinyl sponsor, Ukio Bankas, in the centre. The back of the shirt has the official Sporting ID Scottish SPFL white numbers and name set. Balogh's squad number was one in 2009/10. He wore number 12 in 2008/09.

H.M.F.C.
BALOGH
1
SPL
SCOTTISH PREMIER LEAGUE

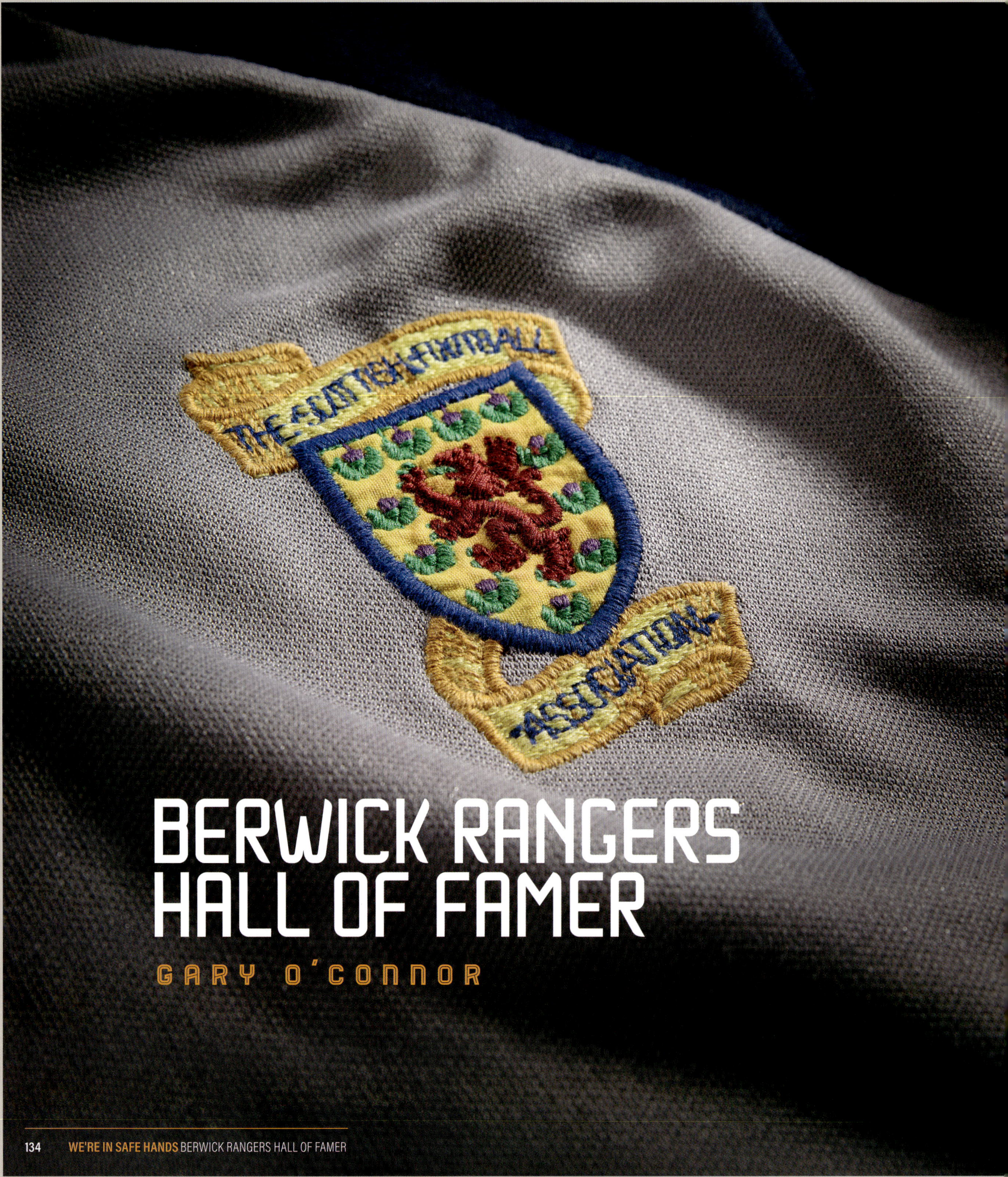

BERWICK RANGERS HALL OF FAMER

GARY O'CONNOR

1988-90 – 1995/96

In the world of football there are players who, despite not making the cut at the highest level, go on to have remarkable careers with other clubs. Former Hearts player Gary O'Connor is one such individual.

In 1990, a young O'Connor signed a Youth Training Scheme (YTS) contract with Hearts. During his second year, he was loaned out to Dalkeith Thistle. Upon completing the YTS, he signed a professional contract for two years. In 1993 he joined Berwick Rangers on an 'unofficial' loan deal, only to return to Gorgie in February 1994. Gary shone at the youth level, representing Scotland at under-16, under-19 and under-21 levels. During his time at Berwick, he was the only player to have played at a currently recognised international level.

Also, during 1990, O'Connor was selected for Scotland's under-16s to play in Norway, alongside Tommy Harrison and Christian Dailly. He established himself in the squad, playing in Belgium, the Netherlands, Italy and France. He then went on to play in the UEFA Under-16 European Championship, though Scotland unfortunately exited at the group stages.

In 1991, O'Connor represented Scotland at under-18 level. He played at Easter Road in a UEFA European Under-18 Championship match against the Republic of Ireland, with the visitors recording a 2-1 victory. Hearts were well represented that evening with team-mates Andy Wright, Tommy Harrison and Anthony Smith also featuring.

O'CONNOR'S HEARTS CAREER PEAKED DURING THE 1995/96 SEASON, WHERE HE MADE THREE COMPETITIVE APPEARANCES AND WAS AN UNUSED SUBSTITUTE 16 TIMES.

A year later, O'Connor was called up for Scotland's under-19s while on the books of Berwick Rangers. He headed to Italy along with some familiar names such as Gary Bollan, Barry Laverty and Andy McLaren. The team was managed by Craig Brown at the time. The game was played in Livorno with Scotland losing 2-0. O'Connor replaced Hibs' Jason Gardiner at half-time with the score at 1-0.

The following year with O'Connor back at Hearts he, Gary Locke and Allan Johnston had to cut short their end-of-season tour to Canada to join the Scotland under-21 squad for the prestigious Toulon Tournament in France. Although O'Connor didn't win a cap during the tournament, he gained invaluable experience that prepared him for the rigours of a professional career at Hearts.

O'Connor's Hearts career peaked during the 1995/96 season, where he made three competitive appearances and was an unused substitute 16 times. His appearances came during a period of transition, with new manager Jim Jefferies eager to freshen up the squad. The season began with Henry Smith and Craig Nelson featuring in both league and cup matches, followed by O'Connor in goal against Kilmarnock, Raith Rovers and Rangers. Jefferies then decided to bring in former French international Gilles Rousset, who became a mainstay from his debut against Falkirk in a league match at Brockville on 28 October 1995.

umbro

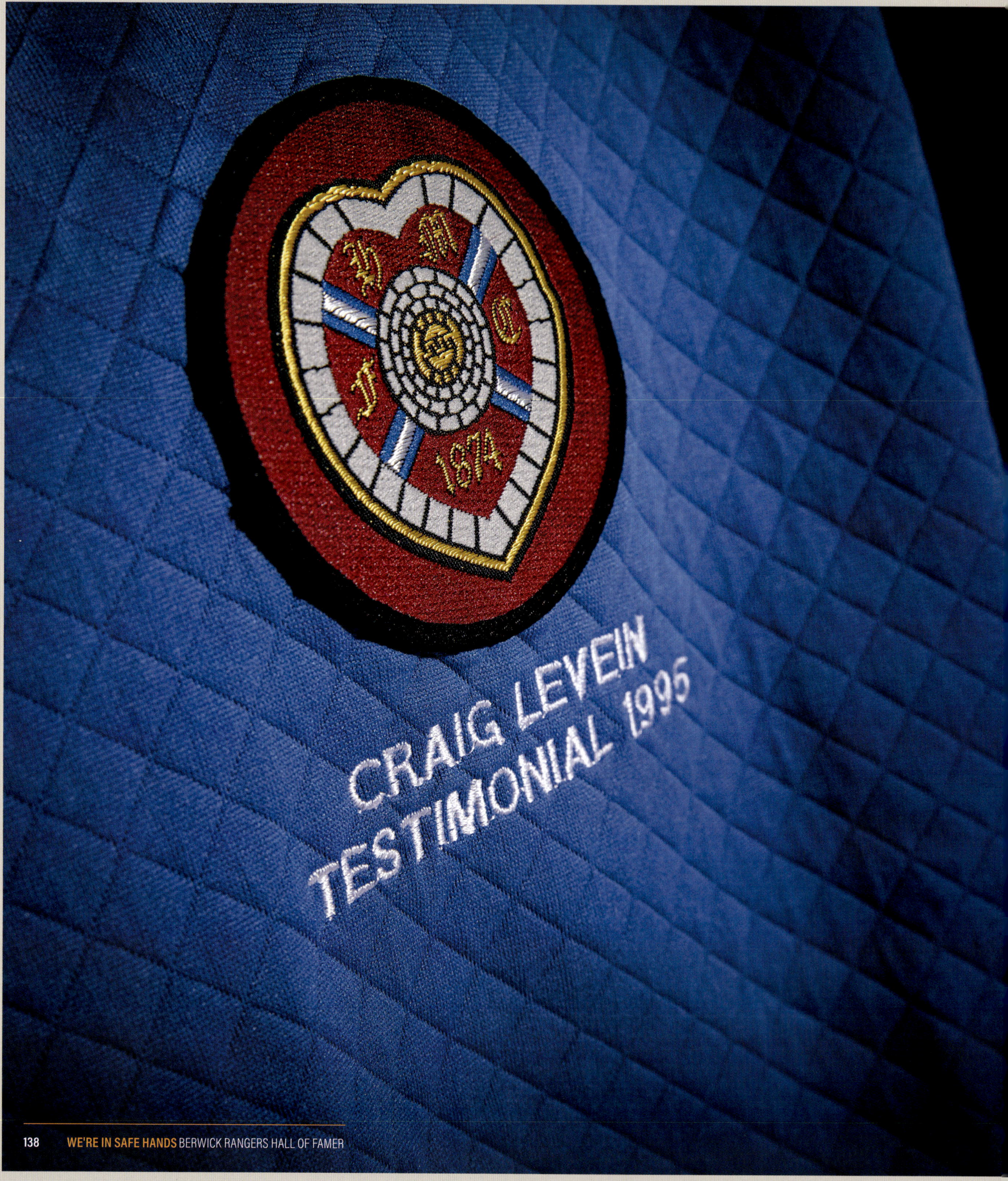
1874
CRAIG LEVEIN
TESTIMONIAL 1995

THIS SHIRT WAS WORN BY GARY WHEN HE WAS A SUBSTITUTE FOR CRAIG LEVEIN'S TESTIMONIAL MATCH AGAINST COVENTRY CITY ON 8 OCTOBER 1995.

O'Connor left Hearts in January 1996, joining Doncaster Rovers for £25,000. He is best known in football circles for his time at Berwick Rangers, making 107 appearances and being inducted into their Hall of Fame in 2016. During his time at Berwick, he played against the likes of England great Paul Gascoigne, trained alongside Scotland stopper Craig Gordon and had an incredible six different spells at Shielfield Park – including one in the heroic Third Division-winning side of 2007.

I have featured two shirts worn by Gary. One is from his Scotland under-16 and under-17 days, produced by Umbro and worn from 1988 to 1990. It's the Scotland home goalkeeper shirt, probably best remembered for being worn in all three group games in the 1990 World Cup in Italy by Jim Leighton. It was an odd choice at the time, given the heavy amount of yellow in the shirt and that of group rivals Sweden and Brazil who also both wore yellow shirts. I was lucky enough to acquire this shirt directly from Gary.

The second shirt was worn by Gary when he was a substitute for Craig Levein's testimonial match against Coventry City on 8 October 1995. Gary was most likely glad that he watched the game from the bench as City ran out 5-1 winners on the day. The shirt was manufactured by Pony and was the away version for 1995/96. It is a

MANUFACTURED BY PONY, THIS WAS THE AWAY SHIRT FOR THE 1995/96 SEASON.

simple and unfussy design with a blue body, black collar and sleeves which have very small blue squares entwined throughout the whole of the shirt. The sponsor logo for the league season was Strongbow but for this one-off game, local company Lothian Plumbing Supplies sat pride of place on the jersey. The Pony logo is placed centrally below the collar in black, with the club badge on the right. Directly under the badge are the embroidered game details 'Craig Levein Testimonial 1995'. On the back is the Pony flock number 17 in white. The shirt was used lightly in 1995/96 with Gilles Rousset preferring the home yellow and black top. The blue shirt was worn at least twice when Hearts visited Celtic Park in the league.

2018–20

A MEMORABLE WARM-UP

ZDENEK 'BOBBY' ZLAMAL

Zdeněk 'Bobby' Zlámal will for ever be remembered by Hearts fans for his rather unusual warm-up routines. Perhaps he was a big fan of another larger-than-life goalkeeper, John Burridge, who was also keen on unique pre-match rituals.

Supporters arriving early at any ground would witness the giant keeper putting himself through a series of cartwheels, handsprings and backflips. These acrobatics prepared Zlámal for action and caused more than a few raised eyebrows in the process.

In an interview, he explained, 'I have warmed up like this since my childhood. When I was younger, I participated in gymnastics alongside football and other sports. I've carried this warm-up routine with me throughout my career. It doesn't matter to anyone else; it's just for me and my confidence. I do this before every game.'

But it wasn't just his warm-up routine that stood out; Zlámal's rather Scottish-sounding nickname sparked curiosity. He clarified, 'My nickname is Bobby because my actual first name is a little challenging for people outside the Czech Republic to pronounce. Interestingly, my uncle, a famous goalkeeper in the Czech Republic especially at Slavia Prague, resembled Bobby Charlton due to his lack of hair. Hence, he was called Bobby Zlámal.'

Bobby had long desired a move to the UK and, when Hearts made contact, he wasted no time. Seeking advice, he turned to Tynecastle legend Rudi Skácel, who recommended them a club with passionate fans and sold-out home matches. Zlámal's dream was to play in Britain and when the offer came, he eagerly accepted. Signing a three-year contract in May 2018, he joined his 15th club.

HEART AND SOUL

Over the next three seasons Zlámal made 53 competitive appearances , 40 of which were in his first season. His competitive debut was against Cove Rangers in a 2-1 win at the Balmoral Stadium in the League Cup group stages. That 2018/19 season also included a Scottish Cup Final appearance at Hampden, where Hearts narrowly lost 2-1 to Celtic. One of Bobby's finest saves in my opinion came in the semi-final against Inverness Caledonian Thistle. With the game finely balanced at 1-0 to Hearts he spectacularly tipped a Joe Chalmers free kick on to the crossbar. That seemed to spur his team-mates on and in the end led to a comfortable 3-0 victory.

In 2019/20 Zlámal managed 13 competitive appearances, while Joel Pereira featured in 25 matches. However, in his final season, Zlámal faced competition from Craig Gordon and found himself out of the first team completely.

But Zlámal's story with Scottish football didn't end there And He sat on the St Johnstone bench as an emergency loan signing during their Scottish Cup semi-final win against St Mirren in May 2021. Invited back for the final against Hibs, Zlámal contributed to St Johnstone's historic cup double in manager Callum Davidson's debut season.

Fast forward to May 2024 and Zlámal made headlines once again. After his contract expired in 2020/21, he unexpectedly announced his retirement from professional football. However, at 38 years old, he made a surprising return, this time as an outfield player.

At the time of writing he was playing for FC Sigma Hodolany in the lower leagues of Czech football. Making his debut as a striker, in a thrilling 4-4 draw with FC Kralice na Hane he scored three goals, including a penalty and an 89th-minute strike. The opposition managed to equalise with their own penalty in the 94th minute.

Interestingly, former Czech Republic star Marek Heinz – still playing at 46 – also scored for Zlámal's side. In response to a fan's comment that he'd been wasted as a goalkeeper, Zlámal humorously replied, 'The gospel truth. The idea of where I could be literally scares me.'

Bobby Zlámal: for ever unconventional, for ever memorable. Never change, Bobby.

The home goalkeeper shirt for the 2018/19 season was designed by Umbro. It features a bold and vibrant yellow body with a subtle bright orange pattern running from the shoulders to the cuffs. It has a classic crew neck design and is made from lightweight, breathable fabric to ensure maximum comfort for the goalkeeper. The Umbro logo is prominently displayed on the left of the chest, while the Hearts club crest is proudly positioned on the right. The shirt also features the Save the Children sponsor logo across the front. This was Bobby's Remembrance shirt that was worn against Kilmarnock on 10 November 2018. The shirt has an embroidered poppy in the centre of the shirt with the wording 'Lest We Forget 1918–2018' under it. Everton's Jordan Pickford wore the same style of shirt the same season in green, as did the keepers of West Ham and Hull City among others. Huddersfield and Derby County also had the same version of shirt but in shades of purple.

The next shirt is from 2019/20, again designed by Umbro. Again, it was a template design featuring a bold, geometric pattern with contrasting colours, making it visually striking. Hearts chose a dark blue body and sleeves with the geometric patterns in black and a lighter blue. Just like the season before, the Umbro logo is prominently displayed on the left of the chest, while the club crest is proudly positioned on the right. The shirt also features the Save the Children sponsor logo across the front. This was Bobby's match-prepared Remembrance shirt when he was on the bench against St Mirren on 9 November 2019. The shirt has an embroidered poppy in the centre of the shirt with the wording 'We Will Remember Them' above it.

This shirt was worn, among others, by Everton with a green version, Bournemouth with yellow, and orange for Burnley and Schalke.

umbro
GB USA ASIA EUR
XL XL XXL XL

PART OF THE ROMANOV REVOLUTION

STEVE BANKS

Englishman Steve Banks made his Hearts debut on 2 October 2005 in a 2-2 league draw with Falkirk at the Falkirk Stadium. It was an unexpected yet interesting first outing for the seasoned shot-stopper. The match saw Hearts drop their first points of the season; Steve came on for Craig Gordon who was red carded after bringing down Bairns striker Darryl Duffy in the box, conceding a penalty.

2006/07

Striker Michal Pospíšil was replaced by Banks, whose first touch was to pick the ball out of the net when Duffy successfully converted from the spot. On the day, Hearts skipper Steven Pressley played a major role in three of the four goals scored. He scored the second of Falkirk's goals in the 68th minute after his attempted header back to Banks was chased down by Duffy, who got to the ball first. His shot was blocked but rebounded back off Pressley and into the net to make it 2-0. Elvis quickly made up for the error when he scored his second goal, picking up a loose clearance and steering home a right-footed shot. He then scored the equaliser in stoppage time in a very similar fashion, latching onto a poor clearance and side-footing the ball into the net. After the game Gordon revealed his disappointment at being sent off as he had hoped to reach the milestone of playing in 100 games in a row against Celtic two weeks later. Gordon also took the time to praise Banks for coming on in difficult circumstances and performing so well. It was the first of three appearances in the 2005/06 season for Steve.

Banks was again used sparingly in 2006/07, making just six appearances. It wasn't until the departure of Gordon to Sunderland for £9m that Steve was fully utilised by the club. He made 32 appearances in 2007/08.

As was the usual at this point of the Romanov era there were some strange goings on at the club. Steve was left out of the team at Kilmarnock on 27 October 2007 after playing ten games in a row. The official line was that he was rested due to overwork. Banks had taken on coaching duties at Tynecastle as well as playing in goal and it was felt he should be given a well-earned break from the firing line and a welcome day's rest. Anthony Basso was given the nod with Eduardas Kurskis on the bench. Likeable Frenchman Basso sadly passed away at the very young age of 45 in March 2025.

Ironically Hearts lost 3-1 that day at Rugby Park in a lacklustre display. Banks, although not between the posts, would bizarrely be involved. As the clock ticked down, Banks was the central figure in the away dugout and the man in charge of the first team. Why? When coach Steve Frail was sent to the stand for an

BANKS
SPL
SCOTTISH PREMIER LEAGUE
SPL
SCOTTISH PREMIER LEAGUE

THIS SHIRT, AS FAR AS I AM AWARE, WAS ONLY WORN AGAINST SPARTA PRAGUE IN A UEFA CUP QUALIFIER AND THEN APPEARED AGAIN WHEN STEVE WORE IT AGAINST DUNFERMLINE IN THE SCOTTISH CUP AT EAST END PARK ON 3 FEBRUARY 2007.

altercation with referee Willie Collum and fourth official Brian Winter, main men Anatoliy Korobochka and Angel Chervenkov were nowhere to be seen. It was left to poor Banks to try to steer the rudderless ship through the final painful minutes; another strange moment for the fans to talk about in the pub after the game.

The following season, Steve, like many other players in that era, fell victim to club owner Vladimir Romanov. He started the first league game, a 3-2 victory at home to Motherwell, which would also be his last appearance for the club. Jamie MacDonald found himself in goal the following week against Rangers at Ibrox. The Evening News reported that the majority shareholder entered the away dressing room at Ibrox moments after the final whistle and claimed to have lost faith in Banks, who was replaced by MacDonald.

'Banks cannot be trusted, the same as [Steven] Pressley could not be trusted, the same as [Andy] Webster could not be trusted,' said Romanov in front of a bemused first-team squad. A meeting between the pair on Saturday morning confirmed Banks's fate; he was demoted to train with the youth team and eventually left for Dundee United in the summer of 2009. Steve played 42 competitive games for Hearts and kept 14 cleans sheets, with a concession rate of 1.26 goals per game. He faced seven penalties and conceded them all.

He left the club with a Scottish Cup winners' medal, having been on the bench for the game against Gretna in May 2006. This set an enviable trend for Steve as he picked up two more Scottish Cup winners medals during his career; he was on the bench for Dundee United's 3-0 win against Ross County in 2010. Steve did it again with St Johnstone when he was on the bench for the Saints 2-0 win against Dundee United in 2014. So, next time you watch a Scottish Cup Final, remember the enigmatic goalkeeper who etched his name into the annals of the game, without even making a save in those decisive moments! Despite the circumstances of his departure from Gorgie, Steve is on record as saying he thoroughly enjoyed his time with Hearts. Quite a journey for the popular Englishman.

This shirt, as far as I am aware, was only worn against Sparta Prague in a UEFA Cup qualifier and then appeared again when Steve wore it against Dunfermline in the Scottish Cup at East End Park on 3 February 2007.

It was made by Hummel, founded originally in Germany in 1923 but becoming a Danish company in 1956. Translated, Hummel is German for bumblebee. The geometric Hummel logo represents a stylised bumblebee and is displayed on shirt sleeves and often appears on the shorts.

They produced kits for Heart of Midlothian for the 2005/06 and 2006/07 seasons. The famous Hummel chevrons appear in black and white flock down the sleeves and have 3D heat-press flock Bank of Scotland Premier League sleeve badges. The club badge as well as the manufacturer's logo is centrally located. The shirt sponsor was Ukios Bankas. The body of the kit is grey with a matching black round-neck collar and cuffs. The standout feature for this shirt is the black polka dots which run from the shoulder to the armpits on each side of the shirt as well as at the bottom of the sleeves above the cuffs. The back of the shirt has official SPL oversized player-issue letters and numbers made by Sporting ID.

STILL GAME

JACK HAMILTON
& VIKTOR NORING

2012/13 – 2016/17

As a fan of the long-running comedy show Still Game, I couldn't resist referencing two of my favourite characters, Jack Jarvis and Victor McDade alongside a Hearts' dynamic duo, Jack Hamilton and Viktor Noring. These two keepers, much like their comedic counterparts, brought excitement and drama to thousands of Hearts fans during their careers with the club.

Hearts signed Swedish stopper Noring from Danish club Lyngby BK in July 2016. This wasn't his first foray into Scottish football as he had spent five months on loan to Celtic from Malmö in January 2013, without making an appearance. He would be joined in the summer of 2016 by Conor Sammon, Faycal Rherras, Robbie Muirhead and Nikolay Todorov. After putting pen to paper on a two-year contract, Noring was quoted as saying, 'The way I'm playing as a keeper, it suits me playing in Scotland. Playing physical suits me well. That was the main reason I wanted to come back [(]after spending time with Celtic], because the country suits me, and the people are very kind. And the football is very good too.' Manager Robbie Neilson added, 'We think he can challenge Jack Hamilton for the number one spot and that's what we want. I want someone to push him on and compete.'

Noring, akin to a new actor stepping onto the stage, made his debut in a friendly against Cowdenbeath at Central Park on 2 July 2016. The understudy that day was none other than current goalkeeping coach Paul Gallacher, fresh from signing a one-year deal as both coach and player. Noring, however, would only feature in three senior games that season, playing the supporting role to 22-year-old homegrown talent Jack Hamilton, who would impressively guard the net 44 times.

NORING'S TENURE AT THE CLUB WOULD LAST FOR 18 MONTHS, ENDING IN MARCH 2018.

Noring's tenure at the club would last for 18 months, ending in March 2018. His performance, like all goalkeepers, was under constant scrutiny. In the modern game even the smallest of errors are magnified. Noring learned this the hard way during his competitive debut against Rangers at Ibrox on 13th of May 2017. Despite a string of excellent saves and a level score thanks to Esmaël Gonçalves's equaliser, a momentary lapse in judgement allowed Barrie McKay to score the winning goal. This incident perhaps marked Noring's card with the Hearts management team, a stark reminder of the unforgiving life of a goalkeeper.

Every player cherishes their professional debut, and Jack Hamilton was no exception. After being recalled from his loan spell at Stenhousemuir, his first appearance was in the first Edinburgh derby outside of the top flight in front of a sell-out crowd at Tynecastle on 17 August 2014. Hearts wore their traditional maroon shirt while Hibs donned their away shirt in the fixture for the first time since 1 December 1985. With the game at a stalemate, Hamilton was adjudged to have fouled Danny Handling in the box leading to a penalty. However, Liam Craig's effort went wide of Hamilton's left-hand post.

The occasion truly came alive in the 75th minute when Sam Nicholson scored a spectacular goal nutmegging Scott Robertson and striking the ball past Mark Oxley from 20 yards. Hearts were awarded a

SPFL
SPFL

ARCHIBALD LEITCH STAND
1914-2017
Save the

HAMILTON WOULD GO ON TO PLAY 63 COMPETITIVE MATCHES FOR HEARTS BEFORE JOINING DUNDEE IN MAY 2018.

penalty on 80 minutes after Robertson fouled Prince Buaben in the box. Willie Collum also showed Robertson his second yellow card for the foul and sent him down the Tynecastle tunnel with the flash of the red card. Buaben confidently blasted his kick high into the left-hand side of the net, making it 2-0 to Hearts. The game saw another red card when Osman Sow was sent off for an elbow incident with Michael Nelson. Hibs managed a consolation goal in the 91st minute through Farid El Alagui, but at the final whistle Jack was swamped by his team-mates, their congratulations ringing in his ears and even a getting hug from the manager. A dream debut for the young keeper, extending Hibs' sequence to just three wins in 22 against their city rivals. The result also laid down an early marker in the promotion race which Hearts would win at a canter. After the game, Robbie Neilson said about the young keeper, 'I thought Jack did very well and I didn't have any doubts about putting him in. I worked with him last year and he's well respected in the dressing room. That tells you a lot about a player. If they've got good ability and something about them then their team-mates respect them.' Hamilton would go on to play 63 competitive matches for Hearts before joining Dundee in May 2018.

When Jack and Viktor were getting game time for Hearts, the club's shirt manufacturer was Puma. Puma is a well-known sportswear company based in Herzogenaurach, Germany.

THIS SHIRT IS A MATCH-PREPARED ONE BELONGING TO JACK HAMILTON FROM 2012/13.

The company was founded in 1948 by Rudolf Dassler, after Dassler split from his brother Adi Dassler, who went on to found adidas. Newcastle United and Arsenal both wore Puma shirts in season 2016/17 and the goalkeeper's shirt, although not identical, had similar patterns: square blocks of vivid blue, pink or yellow blocks in the sleeves.

The first shirt though is a match-prepared one belonging to Jack Hamilton from 2012/13. A young Jack would spend the season as understudy to Jamie MacDonald. The shirt is from adidas and is mainly fluorescent orange. It has a black round neck with matching black sleeves from the elbow down as well as large black cuffs. There is a black block panel running down the sides of the shirt for continuity. The famous adidas three stripes in white, runs from the neck all the way to the bottom of the sleeves. All in all, a decent template from adidas. The template was also worn by Sunderland and Hull City among others that season.

The second shirt was also worn by Jack, this time against St Johnstone on 5 November 2016. The game ended in a 2-2 draw in front of a crowd of 16,421. This luminous yellow shirt features black running across the shoulders and down the length of the sleeves and cuffs. The Puma logo, also in luminous yellow, contrasts against the black on the sleeves accompanied by the vinyl Ladbrokes Premiership sleeve badges. The sponsor for the season was Save the Children. What makes this shirt unique is its Remembrance design

SPFL
SCOTTISH PROFESSIONAL
FOOTBALL LEAGUE

HAMILTO

HAMILTON WOULD GO ON TO PLAY 63 COMPETITIVE MATCHES FOR HEARTS BEFORE JOINING DUNDEE IN MAY 2018.

featuring a poppy and the embroidered wording 'REMEMBER the Battle of the Somme 1916–2016'. Hamilton proudly wore number one on the back of the shirt for 2016/17.

The Viktor Noring shirt, also from 2016/17, shares the same design. However, it has its own unique aspect. When Hearts played Aberdeen at Tynecastle on 7 May, the club recognised that it would be the last game in front of the Archibald Leitch Main Stand. This splendid structure had withstood the test of time, but a much-needed new stand would be in place for the following season. The Hearts players wore a shirt to pay tribute to the iconic main stand with memorial stitching underneath the round neck collar. This was the bench-worn shirt belonging to Noring, featuring his number 13 squad number on the back.

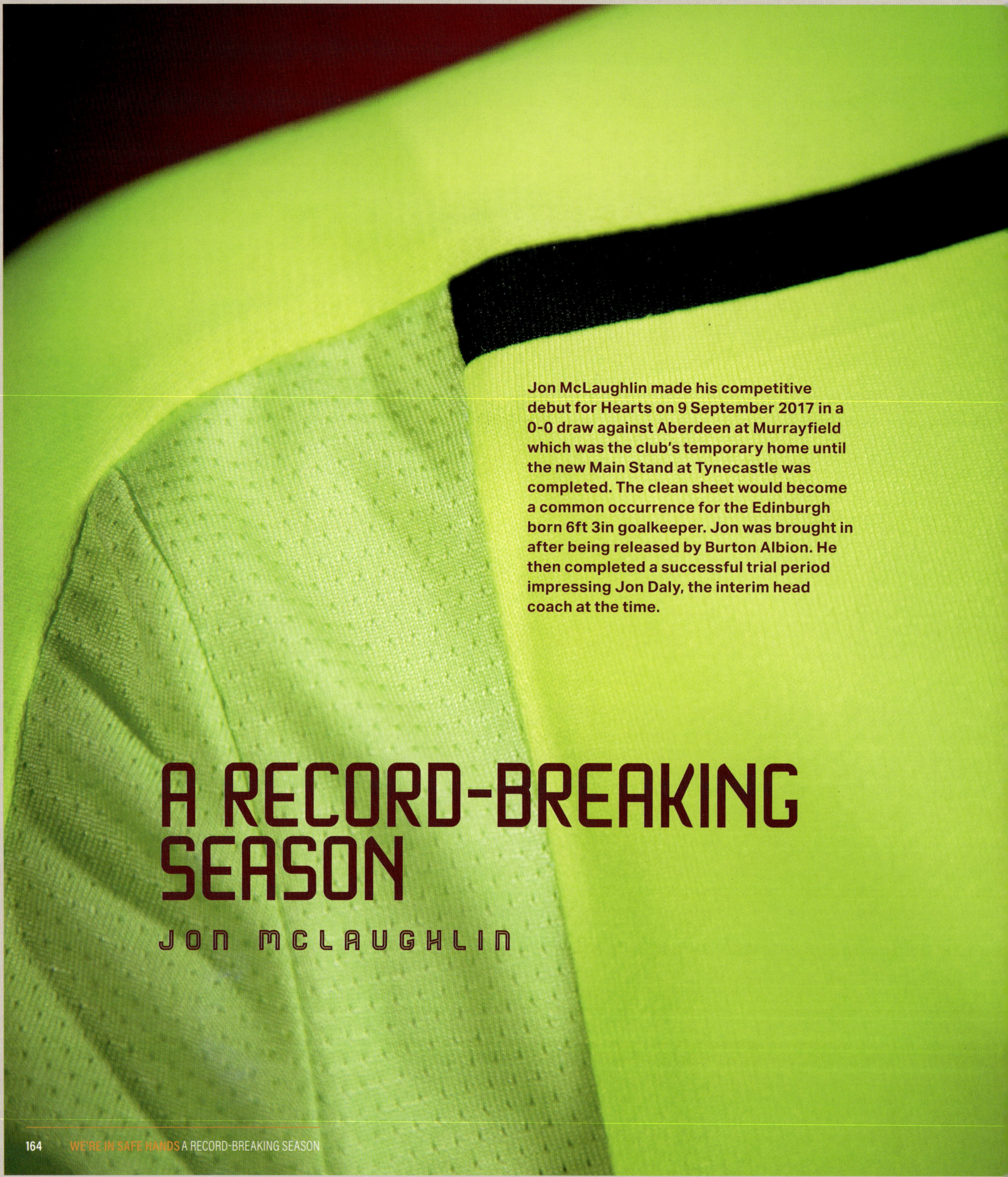

Jon McLaughlin made his competitive debut for Hearts on 9 September 2017 in a 0-0 draw against Aberdeen at Murrayfield which was the club's temporary home until the new Main Stand at Tynecastle was completed. The clean sheet would become a common occurrence for the Edinburgh born 6ft 3in goalkeeper. Jon was brought in after being released by Burton Albion. He then completed a successful trial period impressing Jon Daly, the interim head coach at the time.

A RECORD-BREAKING SEASON

JON MCLAUGHLIN

2017/18

Jon had brought him in as competition for Jack Hamilton and Viktor Noring. McLaughlin told Hearts TV immediately after signing, 'I'm really pleased and obviously really looking forward to playing for a massive club like this. It's my hometown so it's a fantastic feeling and it's been great to be training with the lads for a few days, and I'm now just looking forward to getting on with the serious work.' He went on to say, 'You always want to be at clubs where you're competitive and you're looking to achieve things.' He would certainly do that!

Jon's move to Hearts might have surprised his immediate family members as the majority were Hibs supporters. On revealing the news of his transfer he laughed at his family's reaction, saying, 'When I told them I was coming to Hearts my parents were made up for me — but I wasn't getting too many phone calls back from some of the uncles! They're more diehard!'

'When the derby comes around, I think there will be a few family members in the away end, giving me stick!

'I played against Hibs' under-20s last week and we won 4-1 – yeah, it was nice of them to chuck me into that one straight away just to test me and make sure there was no old affiliation still there! I showed that I'd burnt all the bridges, I suppose!'

Jon would play five times against our city rivals – winning two, drawing one and losing two.

He will always be remembered for eclipsing other Hearts goalkeeping greats such as Jim Cruickshank, Henry Smith and Craig Gordon, by becoming the first in the club's history to keep eight successive clean sheets in 2017/18. Before this Hearts had managed to keep five consecutive clean sheets in 1905,1921, 1936, 1973, 1988, 1991, 1993 and 2010. In 2020/21 and 2021/22 Craig Gordon would go on to beat Jon's record, but more on that later!

Jon's record-breaking sequence was:

Motherwell (H), 1-0
Premiership, 9 December 2017

Dundee (H), 2-0
Premiership 12 December 2017

Celtic (H), 4-0
Premiership, 17 December 2017

St Johnstone (A), 0-0
Premiership, 23 December 2017

Hibernian (H), 0-0
Premiership, 27 December 2017

Aberdeen (A), 0-0
Premiership, 30 December 2017

Hibernian (H), 1-0
Scottish Cup fourth round, 21 January 2018

Hamilton (A), 3-0
Premiership, 24 January 2018

The run cruelly came to an end in the 96th minute at home against Motherwell on 27 January. A Curtis Main header squirmed over the line, and he became the first person to score against Hearts in 830 minutes of football. Reflecting on the great achievement, Jon was quoted as saying, 'I'll always be the first to say that I couldn't have done this on my own and in some of those games I had nothing to do. The defence have left me a spectator on occasions.' He went on to say, 'It's fantastic for myself but it's not about individual plaudits because it's the way we play as a team and a unit. It's a great achievement and you don't get that success if you don't work well as a group and work incredibly hard on the training ground.'

THIS IS OUR STORY · THIS IS OUR SONG

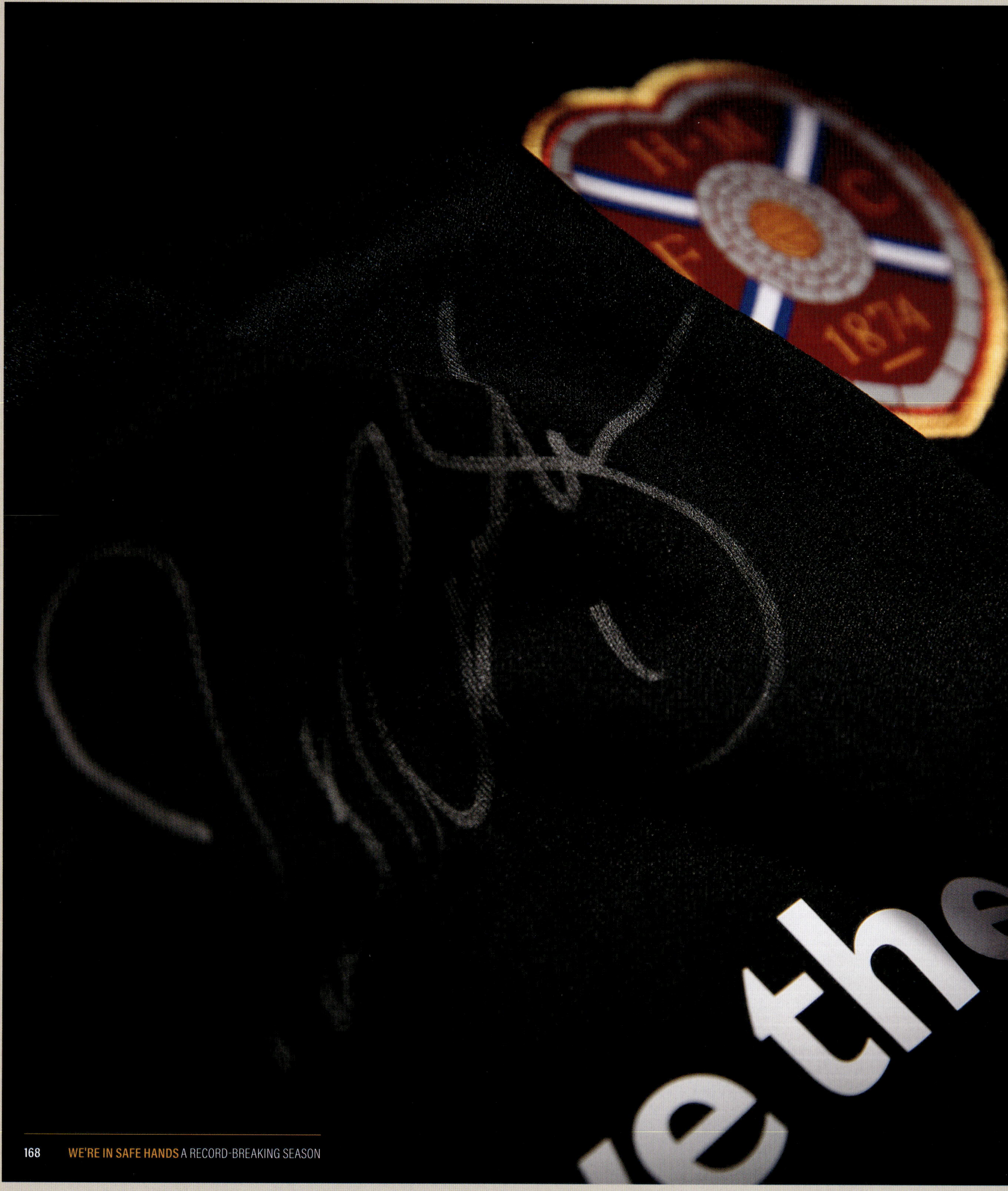

1874

JON WOULD MAKE 36 COMPETITIVE APPEARANCES FOR THE CLUB, ALL IN 2017/18. THE MOST IMPRESSIVE STATISTICS WERE THE 15 CLEAN SHEETS.

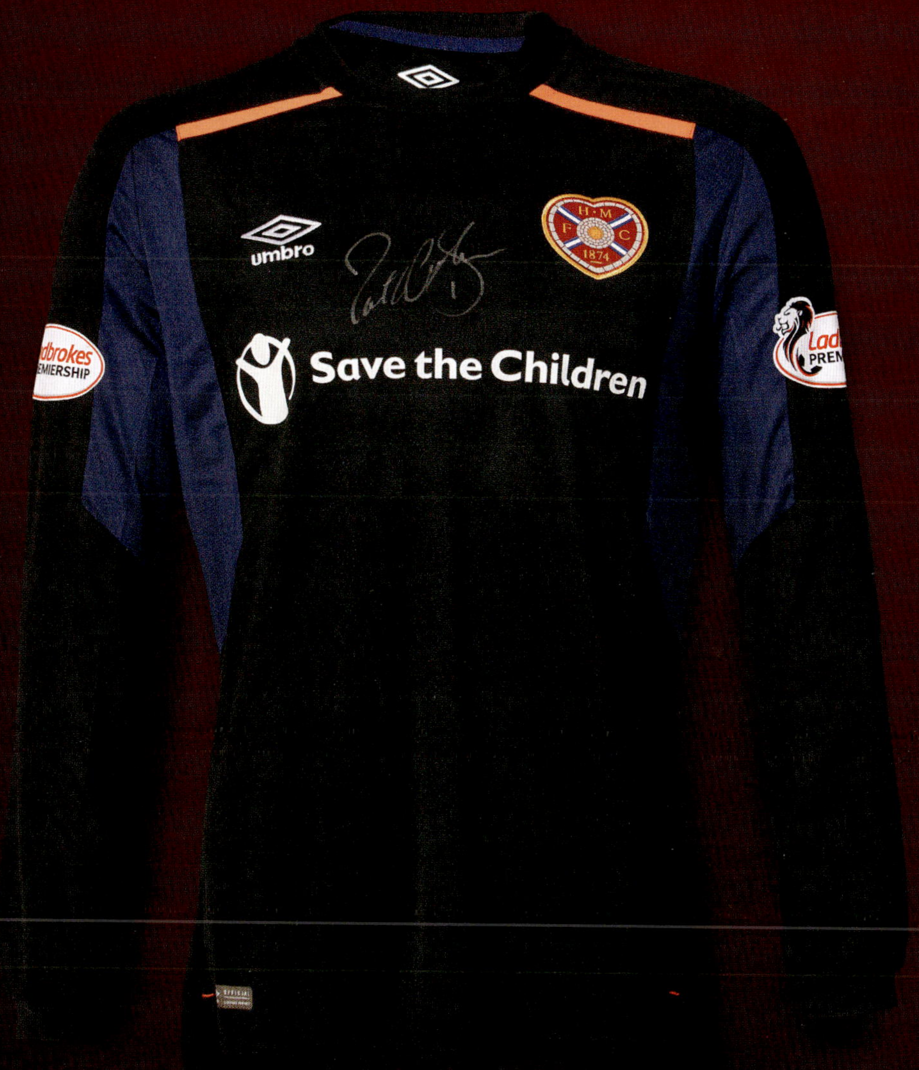

Outside of that sequence of clean sheets, one game in particular emphasised Jon's goalkeeping prowess for me, at home to St Johnstone on 3 February. Hearts won 1-0 thanks to a goal from David Milinković, but the victory was down to the outstanding saves from McLaughlin. The Saints could have easily been 3-0 ahead before half-time. He thwarted everything that they threw at him, including a David Wotherspoon free kick, a one-on-one against Chris Kane and a great save to deny a net bound drive from Scott Tanser and that was just in the first 20 minutes! What an individual performance from a top class keeper.

Jon's outstanding season would lead to an international call up in March 2018 while at Hearts. He was on the bench for the friendlies against Costa Rica and Hungary, and when Scotland visited South America to play friendlies against Mexico and Peru at the end of the season, Jon made his debut against Mexico on 2 June in a 1-0 defeat in front of 70,000 in the famous Azteca Stadium. Unfortunately for Hearts Jon had decided to leave the club by this point and was listed as 'unattached'. He would eventually sign for Sunderland.

The shirt featured was worn against Aberdeen away on 30 December 2017 during that run of results. The shirt is quite unique since it did not feature a sponsor. This was because Hearts wore their navy blue with pink flashes third kit on the day, which did not feature a sponsor for the season.

They would also wear the third kit against Aberdeen and Hamilton in both away games. Jon wore the yellow shirt in all four matches. The team went on to wear it twice more, Partick away in the league and then away against Motherwell in the Scottish Cup. On both these occasions McLaughlin wore the sponsor-less orange version of the shirt.

Jon would make 36 competitive appearances for the club, all in 2017/18. The most impressive statistics were the 15 clean sheets. He will be fondly remembered by Hearts fans as a top-notch goalkeeper.

The first shirt was manufactured by Umbro for the 2017/18 season, featuring a simple yet effective design. The luminous yellow shirt boasts a black trim running from under the collar to the shoulders. Contrasting darker yellow perforated material is used in the armpit and elbow areas, splitting the luminous yellow body. The sleeves are adorned with the vinyl Ladbrokes Premiership sleeve badges. The back of the shirt showcases the Sporting ID number and name set, with Jon's squad number 1. Additionally, the reverse neck of the shirt features a button effect with the famous club mosaic and the Hearts Museum motto – 'This is our story, this is our song'.

The other shirt, also designed by Umbro and worn in 2017/18, is predominantly black. The armpit and elbow areas are highlighted with contrasting dark blue perforated material, splitting the black body. The sponsor, Save the Children, is displayed in white. The sleeves have the vinyl Ladbrokes Premiership sleeve badges and the usual features on the back of the shirt. I found a photograph of Jack Hamilton wearing this shirt against Motherwell at Fir Park on 26 August in his final game for the club. Jon replaced him for the remainder of the season until the last game away to Kilmarnock. Hearts wore their light blue away shirt against Motherwell, and it seems Jon preferred wearing the yellow shirt over the black one. I couldn't find any photographic evidence of Jon wearing the black shirt in a competitive match.

umbro
OFFICIAL
LICENSED PRODUCT

GOTTA CATCH THEM ALL

ROSS STEWART

2021–23

Ross Stewart made his debut for Hearts at Tynecastle against Raith Rovers in the League Cup group stages on 13 October 2020. He had joined in August on a six-month loan deal from Livingston, which was later extended for the season. In May 2021, Stewart signed a two-year permanent deal with the club.

Stewart's arrival coincided with the tumultuous 'COVID' demotion season. The 2019/20 campaign was called early with Hearts last game being an away defeat to St Mirren on 11 March 2020. The league was called off on 13 March, plunging the situation into chaos. Here's a brief timeline of the events that followed:

8 April: The SPFL confirmed a vote to end the lower-division seasons in Scotland and agreed in principle to do the same with the top league. Clubs were given 48 hours to submit their responses.

10 April: Administrative chaos ensued when the SPFL released incomplete results to the media. Dundee initially rejected the proposal in writing which would have defeated the motion but then bizarrely withdrew their response, which the SPFL deemed appropriate.

15 April: After five days of deliberation, which were not afforded to other clubs, Dundee changed their vote to 'yes' and backed the SPFL proposal. This ended the lower league seasons on a points-per-game basis, meaning the Premiership would end the same way.

18 May: An SPFL board meeting confirmed the final placings of the Premiership, effectively relegating Hearts and crowning Celtic as champions.

4 June: The SPFL asked clubs to consider a 14-team Premiership.

15 June: Sixteen of the 42 clubs voted in favour of the proposal.

STEWART'S ARRIVAL COINCIDED WITH THE TUMULTUOUS 'COVID' DEMOTION SEASON. THE 2019/20 CAMPAIGN WAS CALLED EARLY WITH HEARTS LAST GAME BEING AN AWAY DEFEAT TO ST MIRREN ON 11 MARCH 2020.

21 June: Hearts appointed Robbie Nielson as manager; he had previously led them back to the Premiership in 2014/15.

29 June: Hearts legend Craig Gordon returned to Gorgie after a 13-year absence, signing a two-year deal after being released by Celtic. As Hearts and Partick prepared to challenge their premature relegation due to the pandemic in court, Gordon was ready to take the fight onto the pitch.

13 July: The Court of Session in Edinburgh heard Hearts and Partick's case for their relegation to be reversed and ruled it should go to an 'independent' tribunal under SFA rules, effectively sealing both clubs' fate.

28 August: Hearts played their first friendly of 2020/21, against Sheffield United.

6 October: The season began with a 1-0 win over Inverness Caley Thistle in the League Cup group stages.

Ross was on the bench for one of the most anticipated games of the season. Hearts were matched at home against Dundee at Tynecastle for the Scottish Championship-opening fixture on 16 October. The Men in Maroon exacted some revenge and set the tone for the rest of the season with a 6-2 thrashing of their opponents.

He had made his competitive debut in a 3-1 win at Tynecastle against Raith Rovers in a League Cup group game the previous Wednesday. The match saw Craig Wighton score his only hat-trick for the club.

HEARTS
TEWA

umbro

STEWART'S BEST PERFORMANCE ARGUABLY CAME AGAINST CELTIC IN GLASGOW ON 21 AUGUST 2022 AS A DEPLETED HEARTS SIDE BATTLED HARD WITH ROSS PULLING OFF A COUPLE OF FANTASTIC SAVES FROM MATT O'REILLY AND GIORGOS GIAKOUMAKIS.

During his three-season stay, Stewart made nine competitive appearances. His best performance arguably came against Celtic in Glasgow on 21 August 2022 as a depleted Hearts side battled hard with Ross pulling off a couple of fantastic saves from Matt O'Reilly and Giorgos Giakoumakis.

After the final whistle, Robbie Neilson praised the keeper, telling the BBC, 'I thought [Stewart] was great. He's the understudy to Craig Gordon. It gave him the opportunity to come to a big venue against a very good team, and I thought he handled himself very well.'

Ross left Hearts in the summer of 2023 and signed with Partick Thistle in January 2024. During his time at Tynecastle he wore some standout goalkeeper shirts, all produced by Umbro. This set of jerseys are up there as some of my favourites that the club have produced for a long time. The variations created by 'Goggsy the Kitman' over the 2021/22 and 2022/23 seasons are a collector's nightmare. However, tracking down each version is part of the thrill of the chase. It would be quite an achievement to add all the different versions to any collection, if not near impossible!

I have included some of the rarer shirts from this period that I have been fortunate enough to add to my collection.

The first is the away pink shirt with black patterned sleeves from 2021/22, featuring the 'Always Hearts' sponsor on the front. What makes this shirt particularly rare is the lack of evidence that it was ever worn in a game.

The yellow version of this shirt, also sponsored by Always Hearts, was worn during the season by Craig Gordon against Ross County away in September 2021 and April 2022, and it also made an appearance at Livingston in December 2021.

The next shirt follows the same template as the one detailed above but is unsponsored. Its rarity lies in the fact that it is match-prepared with Cinch Premiership and Pawprint sleeve badges, as well as the correct name set and number. However, to my knowledge, it was never worn in a match.

The final shirt belonging to Ross is the same template but with a white body and black patterned sleeves, again with no sponsor. This unsponsored version was rarely seen on the pitch. It appears to have been worn only a couple of times: by Stewart in a pre-season friendly against Ross County in mid-July 2021 and by Gordon against Aberdeen at Pittodrie at the end of October 2021.

For me, the 2021/22 and 2022/23 seasons possibly featured the most variations I have ever seen worn by goalkeepers since I started collecting Hearts shirts. It's very hard to keep track of how many different versions are out there and have been worn in games. To give the reader a flavour, I have attempted to put together a list,

H·M
C
F
1874

TEWA

though it is by no means accurate or exhaustive. If you were a completist it would be quite a feat to, in the words of Pokémon, 'catch 'em all'.

In 2021/22, we had the following variants:

- The yellow shirt had Always Hearts, MND Scotland and unsponsored versions.
- The pink shirt had Always Hearts, MND Scotland and Big Hearts versions.
- The white shirt had unsponsored and MND Scotland versions.

In 2022/23, we had the following variants:

- The grey and orange shirt had MND Scotland, ASC for Gary Locke's testimonial and Big Hearts versions.
- The shirt had unsponsored, MND Scotland and Stellar Omada versions.
- The orange shirt had MND Scotland, a European version with a smaller sponsor and a Stellar Omada version.
- There was also a one-off version of the Umbro yellow and black shirt which was only worn in Europe by Craig Gordon.

That is a lot of variations over two seasons and I'm certain I have not captured them all. I will leave you with a final thought; these variations also include short-sleeved versions which were preferred by Zander Clark and Ross Stewart, as well as the long-sleeved versions worn by Craig Gordon!

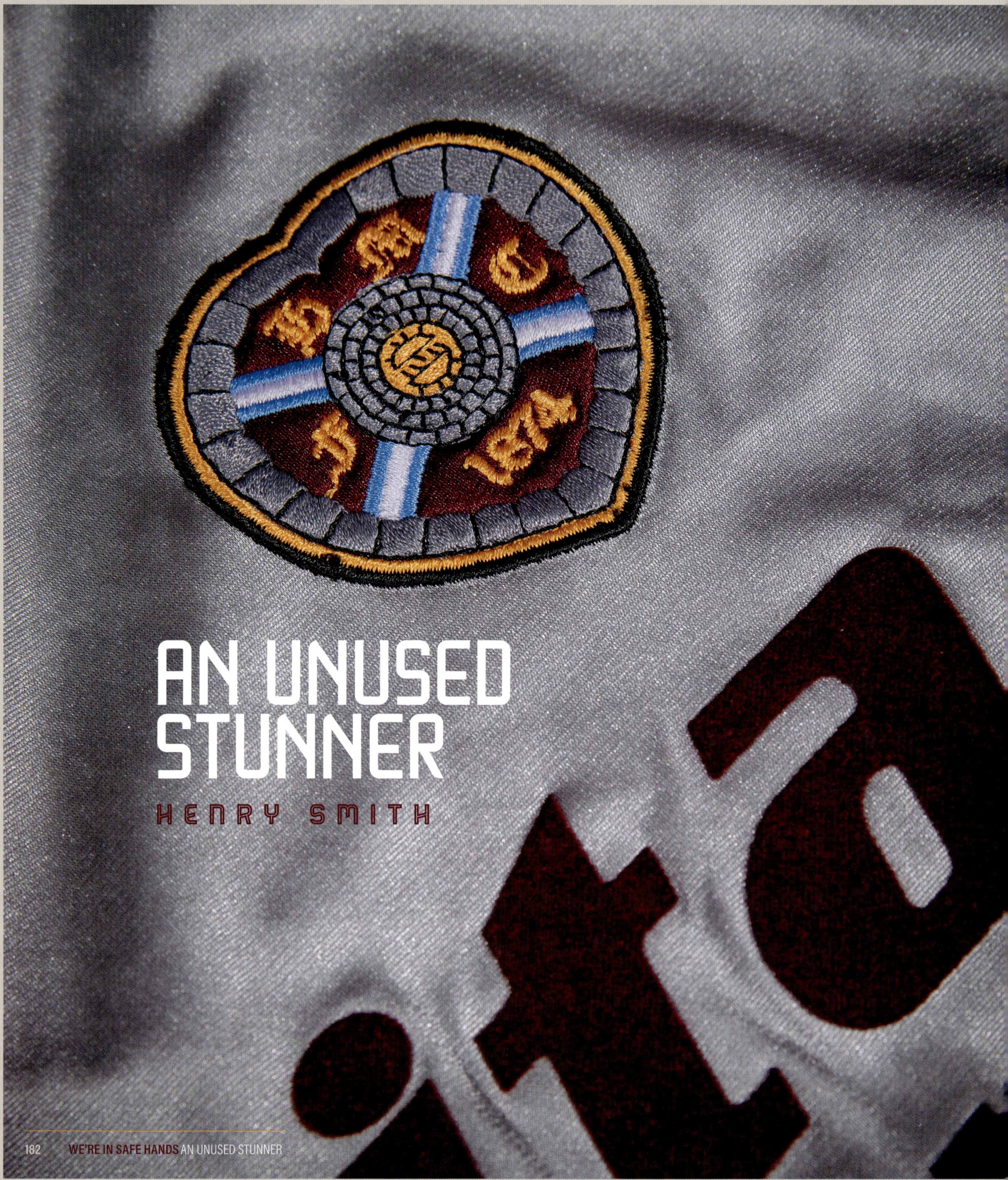

AN UNUSED STUNNER

HENRY SMITH

1987/88

The 1987/88 season was a remarkable one for the club. They finished second to Celtic in the league, trailing the Glasgow side by ten points after the final game. John Robertson netted an incredible 31 goals in all competitions, including 26 in the league. With Hearts performing well across all competitions, fans flocked back to see the Men in Maroon with attendances against Hibs and Celtic notably just under 29,000. The average attendance for the season was 16,633.

The team that season featured some very familiar faces, including three players who each played 51 games: Dave McPherson, Henry Smith and John Colquhoun. They were closely followed in terms of appearances by Brian Whittaker, Gary Mackay and Kenny Black.

There were also some thrilling games that season. Hearts twice notched six goals, winning 6-1 against Kilmarnock in the first round of the League Cup thanks to two goals from Sandy Clark with McPherson, Mackay, Neil Berry and Wayne Foster also finding the back of the net at Tynecastle. The team recorded another six goals when they ran riot at Love Street against St Mirren, with Colquhoun scoring a hat trick, Robbo bagging two and Wayne Foster scoring one. Hearts also recorded a 5-1 away victory against Falkirk at Brockville and a 4-0 win at East End Park against Dunfermline. Goals were plentiful for the fans to enjoy with the team scoring 74 times over a season of 44 games. The season would also see the talismanic John Robertson leave the club for Newcastle United in a record-breaking deal of £750,000 in April 1988.

It wasn't just the forwards who made headlines. Hearts recorded 18 clean sheets in the league and conceded a miserly 32 goals. The defence that season was bolstered by the signing of Dave McPherson and

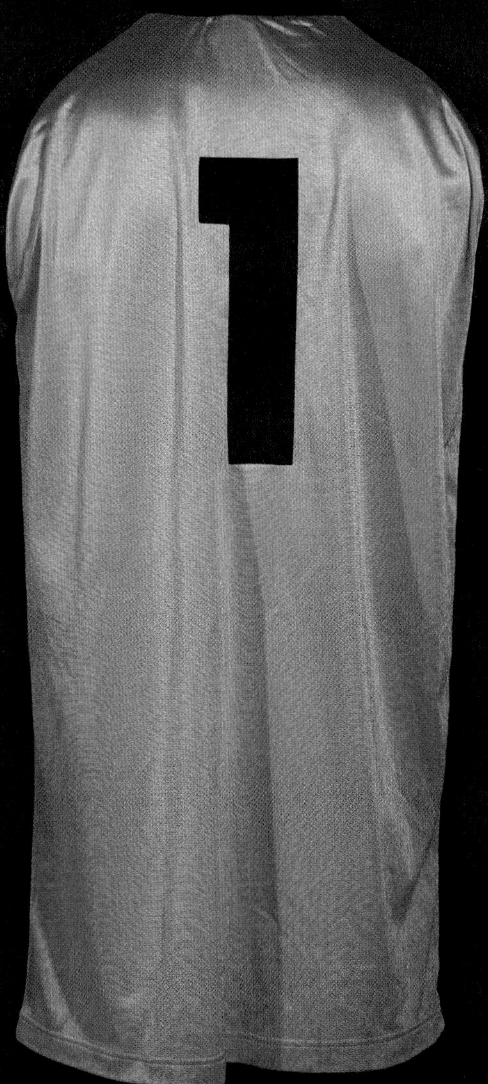

FOR HENRY THE SEASON HAD HIGHS AND LOWS. THE HIGH OF REPRESENTING HIS COUNTRY FOR THE FIRST TIME AND THE LOW OF THE 2-1 DEFEAT TO CELTIC IN THE SCOTTISH CUP SEMI-FINAL ON 9 APRIL 1988.

Hugh Burns from Rangers in a deal worth £500,000. With Henry Smith and Craig Levein, as well as the experienced Brian Whittaker and Sandy Jardine already at the club, they gelled together well. Henry's form would see him sign a new three-year deal.

For Henry the season had highs and lows. The high of representing his country for the first time and the low of the 2-1 defeat to Celtic in the Scottish Cup semi-final on 9 April 1988. Henry, who had been suffering from a thigh injury, inexplicably made two handling errors in the last three minutes of the game which meant Hearts quickly went from 1-0 up to 2-1 down. A day to forget! Co-manager Sandy Jardine backed the big stopper and the day after the game had a heart-to-heart with Henry. He hoped it had made him feel a little better. Sandy told the press, 'Henry was shattered, the tragedy is that Henry has had a magnificent season.' Hearts would gain a little revenge a week later when they defeated Celtic 2-1 in the League at Tynecastle. It would end the Hoops' 31 unbeaten run with Mike Galloway and skipper Gary Mackay bagging the goals for Hearts.

The sparkling form of the whole team saw Mackay, Smith and Colquhoun reap the rewards by each winning caps for Scotland.

The last game of the season was at Tannadice against Dundee United and ended in a 0-0 draw. The Hearts fans with good memories will recall that it would also see a debut for 17-year-old Scotland youth international Alan McLaren, the first of 219 appearances that the classy defender would make for the club. On the day, he also earned the distinction of becoming the final player booked by referee Tommy Muirhead of Stenhousemuir, who was officiating his last game.

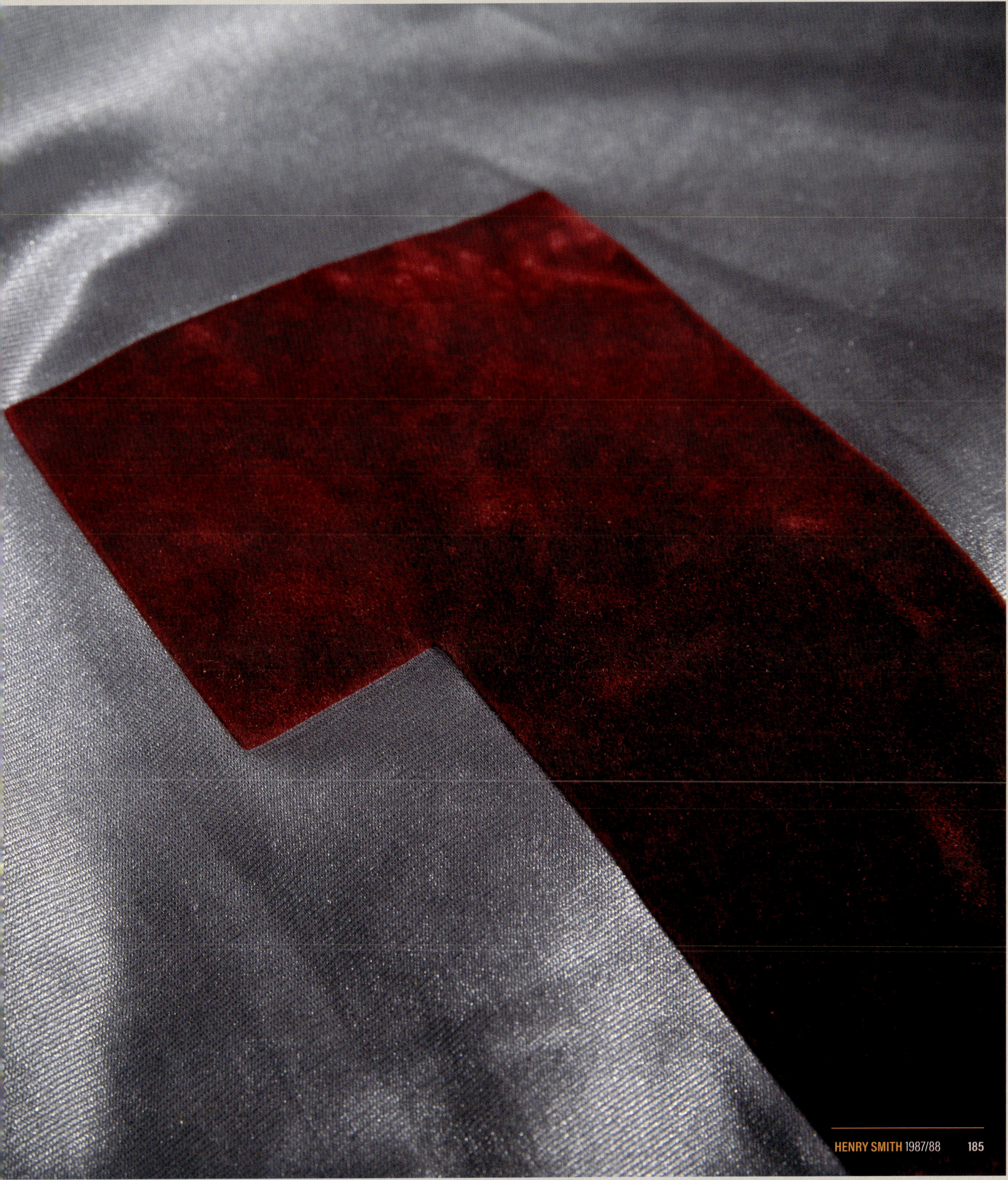

WHY DID HENRY WEAR THE 1986/87 GREY KEEPER SHIRT FEATURING THE MITA SPONSOR RATHER THAN THE CURRENT SEASON GREY SHIRT WHEN HEARTS PLAYED DUNDEE IN A 3-1 WIN AT DENS PARK ON 19 DECEMBER 1987?

But back to Henry. Throughout the season, he consistently wore the black-sleeved and yellow-bodied shirt as well as the grey bodied and black sleeved Bukta keeper's shirt. Smith wore black shorts and matching black socks with the yellow shirt. When wearing the grey version, which was almost the flip of the yellow shirt, he also sported black shorts and socks.

However, throughout any season, there always seemed to be a keeper kit oddity that would confuse a shirt collector like me. As an example, why did Henry wear the 1986/87 grey keeper shirt featuring the Mita sponsor rather than the current season grey shirt when Hearts played Dundee in a 3-1 win at Dens Park on 19 December 1987? Perhaps the yellow shirt clashed with the referee, or his original choice clashed with the Dundee keeper Bobby Geddes.

So, this begs another question about the keeper shirt I have in my collection from season 1987/88. It has the Mita Copiers sponsor which dates it to 1987/88 but appears to have never featured in a competitive match. I have scoured the internet, Hearts Museum scrapbooks as well as my own personal newspaper clippings, but cannot find a single picture of Henry wearing the shirt. In my humble opinion this mystery shirt is a cracker, and I find it very surprising if it was never worn in a game. Perhaps it was a sample that was rejected by the club or by Henry.

The standout features of this shirt are the maroon 'Mita Copiers' sponsor and the matching maroon number on the back. The Bukta logo is in black which is a great contrast to the shiny metallic grey effect body and black padded sleeves with matching collar. This shirt is a real eye-catcher.

The question is, can anybody remember seeing it being worn in a game? It would be great to find out more information on it.

A KEEPER CRISIS

TEPI MOILANEN

2003/04

In the chilly winter of 2002, Hearts faced a goalkeeper crisis. Roddy McKenzie, their trusted shot-stopper, had broken his thumb during the midwinter break in Portugal and the club urgently needed a replacement. Their options were limited: the young and inexperienced Craig Gordon or 16-year-old Lee Windrum. The pressure was on to find a solution.

McKenzie had patiently bided his time, waiting in the shadows behind the legendary Antti Niemi. But fate dealt him a cruel blow when he snapped his thumb just five months after Niemi's departure for Southampton. Ironically, it was Niemi himself who would play a pivotal role in Hearts' search for a new goalkeeper.

Enter Tepi Moilanen, a fellow Finn. Niemi recommended him to Hearts and the club's boss at the time, Craig Levein, decided to follow up on the tip. Levein secured Tepi on loan from Preston North End until the end of the 2002/03 season; Tepi had fallen out of favour at Preston due to the arrival of Scottish international Jonathan Gould from Celtic.

Moilanen became the second Finnish international goalkeeper to don a Hearts jersey, following in Niemi's footsteps. Levein expressed confidence in Tepi, saying, 'Our scouts were impressed with him, and I've spoken to a number of people down in England, including David Moyes, who all believe he'll make a real impact at Tynecastle.'

And make an impact he did: Tepi's solid performances helped Hearts qualify for the UEFA Cup that season. His debut was delayed though. Initially expected to play against Falkirk in the Scottish Cup, Levein opted to give Craig Gordon a chance. Unfortunately for Gordon, an abject team performance

2003/04 BROUGHT MIXED FORTUNES FOR TEPI. HE EARNED A CAP FOR FINLAND IN A FRIENDLY AGAINST HONDURAS BUT THE OUTSTANDING FORM OF CRAIG GORDON EVENTUALLY EDGED HIM OUT AS THE REGULAR GOALKEEPER.

and an inspired Colin Samuel, who scored a hat-trick, led to a heavy 4-0 defeat. Despite the loss, the *Edinburgh Evening News* named Gordon as the star man, praising his composure, kicking and faultless handling.

Tepi's moment arrived soon after as Levein entrusted him with the starting spot against Aberdeen at Pittodrie. It turned out to be a dream start as Hearts secured a 1-0 victory thanks to a Gary Wales goal. Tepi showcased his skills with a couple of excellent saves, even in treacherous conditions.

His performances throughout the season earned him a permanent two-year deal. However, 2003/04 brought mixed fortunes for him. Tepi earned a cap for Finland in a friendly against Honduras but the outstanding form of Craig Gordon eventually edged him out as the regular goalkeeper. Craig featured in 29 of the team's league fixtures.

The 6ft 5in stopper would leave Hearts in the summer of 2005. He returned to his country of birth, joining the superbly named FC KooTeePee as their first-choice goalkeeper.

The keeper shirt featured is from 2003/04 and is the home shirt manufactured by Reebok. The shirt was a template with West Ham, Manchester City and Liverpool all wearing the same model.

A rather stylish combination of vivid orange and blue, it has a white V-neck with black piping running down the grey sleeves ending at a panel just before the cuffs. The body of the shirt features thin tonal double vertical pinstripes within the fabric. Player-worn shirts had a woven club badge and a heat-pressed flock Reebok logo on the front of the shirt. The sponsor as per the previous season was all:sports. It has 3D heat press vinyl Bank of Scotland Premier League sleeve badges. The back of the shirt has official SPL oversized player issue letters and numbers made by Sporting ID.

all-sport

HE ISN'T FINISHED

ANTTI NIEMI

2001/02

Hearts signed the Finnish international Antti Niemi prior to the Edinburgh derby in December 1999. He had been on loan to Charlton Athletic from Rangers and travelled up from London to put pen to paper on a two-and-a-half-year, £400,000 deal. It was reported to be a £250,000 original payment which would rise by a further £150,000 if the talented keeper made a set number of appearances.

Given that Rangers had paid £1.2m to FC Copenhagen two years previous, it looked like Hearts had picked up a potential bargain. The deal was initially seen as Niemi providing cover to Scottish Cup hero Gilles Rousset, who was expected to return to France in the summer. It didn't quite happen that way as Antti would play 21 of the remaining 24 games. His debut was against Hibs at Tynecastle on 19 December in a 3-0 defeat. It's safe to say he wouldn't have particularly enjoyed it, but he was named man of the match for his performance.

Manager Jim Jefferies said, 'We have had an eye on him for some time and thought now was the right time to move. Fortunately, the clubs agreed on a fee and, hopefully, everything will now be tied up with the player. At 27, he is a good age for a goalkeeper and the fact he is an international proves his credentials.'

Antti is remembered fondly by the Hearts supporters and is considered by some as the best keeper to have played for the club.

Likewise, he looks back at his time at Tynecastle with nothing but happiness. He was back in Scotland when Finland played Scotland in a Friendly match on the 7th of June 2024 in preparation for Euro 2024. He shared some memories with the Edinburgh Evening News, saying, 'We had a great dressing room filled with good guys like Steve Fulton and Colin Cameron. The team spirit was fantastic, and I felt that after being at Rangers for two and a half years being second or third choice, I suddenly became a particularly important player for the team.

'YOU REMEMBER YOUR FOOTBALLING DAYS AND HEARTS HAVE ALWAYS BEEN THE CLUB FOR ME. DON'T GET ME WRONG. I WAS LUCKY TO PLAY IN THE ENGLISH PREMIER LEAGUE WITH SOUTHAMPTON AND FULHAM, BUT THERE WAS SOMETHING ROMANTIC ABOUT THE PLACE.'

'I was one of those players that was, not carrying the team, but a senior player that was expected to do well and save points. I really enjoyed the responsibility. Obviously, there are one or two games where I could have done better, but if I played something like 120 games, there were a lot of games where I felt I really contributed to a result. I felt I played a good part, made some good saves and can feel happy with myself. It was almost like a perfect period in my football career. That's how I feel now looking back in the last 20 years. It's been more than 20 years, it's scary. Just overall, I can be proud and if I ever go to Hearts games, I can keep my head high knowing I gave something to this club. It's a great feeling.

'You remember your footballing days and Hearts have always been THE club for me. Don't get me wrong. I was lucky to play in the English Premier League with Southampton and Fulham, but there was something romantic about the place.

'I went there from Rangers where I was second or third keeper and suddenly got the chance to be number one and be a big part of the team.

'We finished third, had some European football, memorable derbies. I hope it doesn't sound cocky, but I really can't remember too many games I let the team down.

'I loved my time there and it's definitely one of those places I miss now and then.'

Ask any Hearts fan to name Antti's best save and they are likely to mention one from Chris Sutton in a league game at Celtic Park in November 2000 against the Hoops. Unsurprisingly, Niemi agrees. In the build-up to the goal, first Henrik Larsson got on the end of Alan Thompson's in-swinging free kick in the 24th minute, but the big Finn produced an acrobatic save to push the striker's header over his crossbar.

But then came the stunning save when Bobby Petta found Sutton in the box and the striker's header looked destined for the corner, but Niemi somehow stretched enough to claw away the effort.

Niemi described it in his own words, 'When the ball left his head, for a brief second I thought well, I'm going to go anyway but it is going to go in. Once you are in the air it was "oh, bloody hell, I might reach this". So, it was surprising to get that, but it was an exceptionally good save, I have to say.

'It was one of those games where you let in a lot of goals and it was one-way traffic, I still think it was one of my best saves ever.'

Antti is also fondly remembered for his great ability as a penalty saver. During his Hearts career, he faced 12 penalties and was only beaten six times. The six that didn't hit the back of the net were:

- **Hearts 2 Celtic 4**, 19 August 2000
  Henrik Larsson missed on 46 minutes
- **Dundee United 1 Hearts 1**, 7 April 2001
  Saved from Charlie Miller
- **Kilmarnock 1 Hearts 1**, 27 April 2001
  Christophe Cocard hit the post
- **Hibernian 0 Hearts 0**, 13 May 2001
  Mixu Paatelainen skied over the bar in the 92nd minute
- **Hearts 2 Dunfermline Athletic 0**, 20 April 2002
  Saved from Scott Thomson
- **Hearts 1 Celtic 4**, 28 April 2002
  Shaun Maloney hit the post in the 91st minute

My personal favourite penalty miss was the derby at Easter Road. In a scrappy game, Hibs had the chance to seal the win when Grant Murray fouled David Zitelli in the box. Niemi's fellow Finn Mixu Paatelainen, who appeared to be the most relaxed man in Leith, casually ballooned a lazy shot over the bar, cueing outrageous celebrations in the away end.

Antti's impressive performances in goal naturally attracted attention and in August 2002, Southampton came knocking. While many players would eagerly seize the opportunity to play in what is often considered the world's top league, Niemi was initially hesitant, highlighting his deep affection for his time at Hearts.

When asked if leaving Tynecastle for the Premier League was tough, he responded, 'Yes, it was. Of course, when Premier League clubs show interest, it's a big deal – even though it wasn't Manchester United, Arsenal or Chelsea, it was Southampton, and I had a fantastic time there.'

The icing on the cake for Niemi was that his last game was in front of a home crowd and was the famous Mark de Vries derby on the 11th of August 2002. Hearts cruised to a 5-1 victory thanks to four goals from Tynecastle debutant de Vries.

Niemi played 106 competitive matches for Hearts, keeping 34 clean sheets and averaging a goals conceded ratio of 1.3 per game.

He retired from football at the age of 36, saying, 'I've got no regrets whatsoever.'

After a chronic wrist injury denied him the chance to regain the goalkeeper's jersey at English Premier League side Fulham, Niemi was quoted as saying, 'I'm proud of what I've achieved in football. I've had a good career in English, Scottish and international football. I got so much more from football than I could have ever wished for and that's the most important thing.' A Finland debutant in November 1992, he earned 67 caps for his country, the last of which came in October 2007. A great goalkeeper.

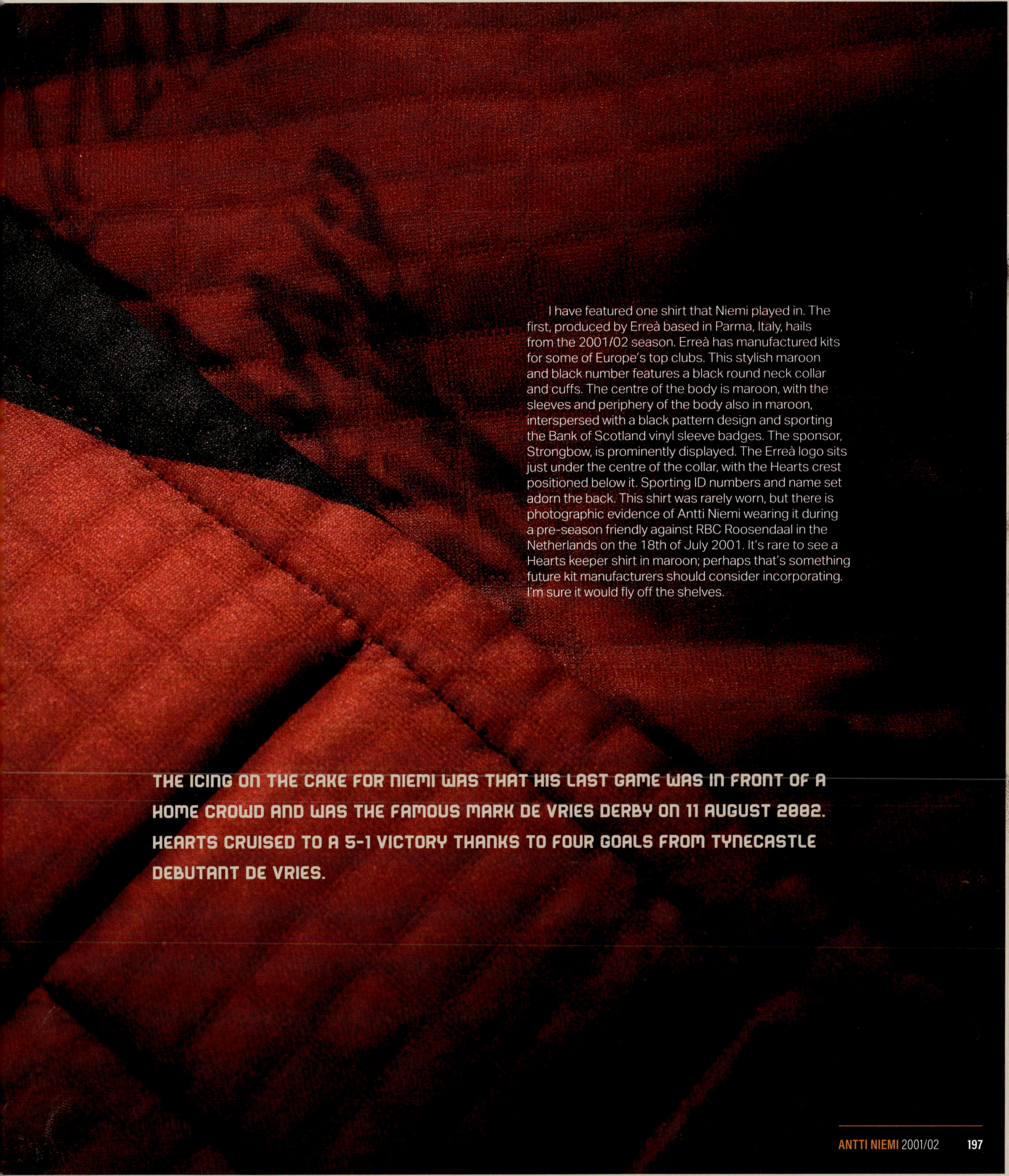

I have featured one shirt that Niemi played in. The first, produced by Erreà based in Parma, Italy, hails from the 2001/02 season. Erreà has manufactured kits for some of Europe's top clubs. This stylish maroon and black number features a black round neck collar and cuffs. The centre of the body is maroon, with the sleeves and periphery of the body also in maroon, interspersed with a black pattern design and sporting the Bank of Scotland vinyl sleeve badges. The sponsor, Strongbow, is prominently displayed. The Erreà logo sits just under the centre of the collar, with the Hearts crest positioned below it. Sporting ID numbers and name set adorn the back. This shirt was rarely worn, but there is photographic evidence of Antti Niemi wearing it during a pre-season friendly against RBC Roosendaal in the Netherlands on the 18th of July 2001. It's rare to see a Hearts keeper shirt in maroon; perhaps that's something future kit manufacturers should consider incorporating. I'm sure it would fly off the shelves.

THE ICING ON THE CAKE FOR NIEMI WAS THAT HIS LAST GAME WAS IN FRONT OF A HOME CROWD AND WAS THE FAMOUS MARK DE VRIES DERBY ON 11 AUGUST 2002. HEARTS CRUISED TO A 5-1 VICTORY THANKS TO FOUR GOALS FROM TYNECASTLE DEBUTANT DE VRIES.

HE'S BETTER THAN YASHIN

JIM CRUICKSHANK

For Hearts fans of a certain age, Jim Cruickshank will always be the best goalkeeper ever to pull on the famous jersey. His performances are still talked about and revered by the supporters.

I've come tantalisingly close to obtaining a shirt that belonged to the legendary stopper, but somehow, a deal has never quite materialised. Perhaps the owners just couldn't bring themselves to part with such an iconic shirt and I totally understand that.

I've been fortunate enough to see three of his shirts close-up: two wonderful Scotland tops including Jim's Scotland debut jersey, both on loan to the amazing Hearts Museum, and Jim's Scottish Cup Final shirt from the 1976 game against Rangers. A striking all-yellow effort from Umbro complete with embroidery, it's a real rarity. A few years back I was lucky enough to meet Willie Gibson, who still has his shirt from that same final. Jim's shirt is in the capable hands of Hearts memorabilia collector Gary Cowan.

Maybe one day I'll be lucky enough to add one of Jim's shirts to my collection.

So, here I am, breaking my own rule by writing a chapter without a match shirt to accompany it. Yet I feel a bit of poetic licence is warranted, especially as my uncles and Hearts-supporting friends at the bowling club would never forgive me if I wrote a book about the club's goalkeepers without mentioning Jim Cruickshank. I'm more than happy to bend the rules this once. I'm sure the wonderful team at Pitch Publishing will help me provide some iconic images of Jim to do him justice.

Between 1960 and 1977 Jim made 544 competitive first-team appearances for Hearts, the fourth-highest tally in the club's history, keeping 140 clean sheets. He faced 78 penalties and saved 21 one of them.

Donald Ford, the former Hearts and Scotland striker who was Cruickshank's team-mate for more than a decade, spoke of his adoration of Jim after his passing in November 2010. 'I think any supporter you spoke to about Jim would struggle to remember a goal he conceded which was as a result of a glaring mistake on his part,' Ford told *The Scotsman*.

'Hearts have been fortunate through the years with some very fine goalkeepers. But I don't think Hearts have had a better goalkeeper than Jim. He was quick off his line, brilliant at getting his angles right and a fantastic shot-stopper. He commanded his penalty area. His attitude was that if the ball was within ten or 12 yards of his line, then it was his. He would knock all and sundry, including his own defenders, out of the way to get it.'

Jim was a Scotland schoolboy international and his goalkeeping prowess was boosted by his talent as a gymnast. His first club was Drumchapel Amateurs. He then signed for Queen's Park in 1959, making 30 first-team appearances for the Hampden residents and being scouted by many clubs. Hearts manager Tommy Walker persuaded Jim to sign professional forms at Tynecastle in May 1960.

He made his first-team debut at 19 in a 1-0 league defeat at Ayr United five months later. He was in esteemed company that day, lining up with Willie Bauld, Gordon Smith and Alex Young. Hearts lost 1-0 but were perhaps a bit unlucky, hitting the woodwork six times! The papers mentioned Jim's debut briefly, noting, 'Cruickshank came too far out of his goal on occasion.'

Initially, Jim had to remain as understudy to Gordon Marshall. He played in the 1961 League Cup Final replay (only his sixth appearance) when Marshall was injured, but at 20, he couldn't prevent a 3-1 defeat to Rangers. Frustrated by limited appearances, Jim walked out of the club in 1963 when Marshall was restored to the first team. Assistant manager Johnny Harvey persuaded him to return and, following

Marshall's surprise move to Newcastle United, Jim was established as Hearts' number one.

Donald Ford again reminisced about his team-mate to the local press, 'Hearts fans will remember him charging out of his penalty area to berate team-mates responsible for conceding a goal. Jim would even hold an inquest into losing a hand of cards on the team bus. That attitude made him a wonderful goalkeeper and a truly great Hearts player.'

Two games stand out for fans thanks to Jim's incredible performances. The first was the new year derby on 2 January 1967 at Tynecastle. Despite Hibs' dominant performance, Jim answered every challenge, including split-second saves from Jimmy O'Rourke and Peter Cormack. Hibs were given a penalty after Alan MacDonald fouled Eric Stevenson. Joe Davis's initial shot was saved by Jim, who then blocked Davis's rebound and foiled Alan McGraw on the third attempt. Goalkeeping at its finest.

The second game was a 0-0 draw against Celtic on 28 March 1970. Known for his hard shot, Celtic's Tommy Gemmell took a controversial penalty. Jim dived to make a stunning save and despite being down to ten men after Jim Townsend's sending-off, Hearts held firm. The *Evening News* hailed Jim as the player of the match, noting that he was regularly 'rising like a hawk to pick the ball off the heads of Celtic attackers, running out to clutch menacing cross balls and saving shots that shouldn't have been saved'.

Jim's popularity was such that the Gorgie faithful honoured him with a song. Not many goalkeepers inspire terracing songs, but Jim did. Fans compared his all-black kit to that of USSR goalkeeper Lev Yashin, singing to the tune of the old hit song 'Ay Ay Ay Ay', 'We all agree, Cruickshank is better than Yashin; Donald Ford is better than Eusébio, And the Hibees are in for a thrashin'.'

Jim made his Scotland debut in a 2-2 draw against West Germany in 1964 but didn't play again until May 1967 against Australia, totalling nine appearances. A standout game was against England at Hampden in April 1970, in front of more than 137,000 spectators. Facing World Cup winners Geoff Hurst and Martin Peters, Jim helped Scotland to a goalless draw, which was the first between the two sides since their inaugural match in 1872.

Donald Ford, in the same interview, picked up on Cruickshank's international career, stating, 'Jim never got the international recognition he deserved. Some people said he was too small, but that was just nonsense. He should have won scores of caps for Scotland.'

Jim sadly left Tynecastle under a cloud in 1977 when the club's relegation from the Premier Division saw him released and a promised testimonial match failed to materialise.

'That was dreadfully unfortunate,' said Ford. 'He really fell out with the club and never let it go. We had an annual golf day every year between former Hearts and Hibs players at Baberton, which Jim Brown and Dave Clunie tried regularly to get Jim along to, but he always refused. But that's the kind of person Jim was. He was never slow to say what he thought and was usually on firm ground when he did so.'

Over the years there are very few Tynecastle greats that enjoyed the level of adoration which Cruickshank received from Hearts fans, showing how revered and loved Jim Cruickshank was down Gorgie way.

REDEMPTION

GILLES ROUSSET

1995/96 – 2000/01

Two months into his first stint at Hearts it was clear to Jim Jefferies that personnel changes had to be made. Jim was appointed in 1995 to ensure the club didn't have to fight another relegation battle like they had in the previous two seasons. He knew that decisions would have to be made that would potentially ruffle a few feathers.

Jefferies left Falkirk having guided them to a fifth-place finish in the Premier League. He had also been very successful in his wheeling and dealing in the transfer market with a limited budget. Jim was going to have to get used to the same model at Hearts if he wanted to drive them up the table. He was also acutely aware, having played for the club for many years, that the expectation levels from fans were very high.

The goalkeeping situation was a particular problem. Club legend Henry Smith was now entering the twilight of his career, backup Craig Nelson hadn't managed to reproduce the form he had shown when at Partick Thistle and the third choice was the young and inexperienced Gary O'Connor. Jim would try them all but neither really grabbed the opportunity with both hands, so he was on the lookout for a keeper. If paper talk at that time was true, Jim had his eye on St Johnstone's Andy Rhodes in a swap deal for midfield stalwart John Millar. John felt he still had a career at Tynecastle and turned down the move, so the search continued.

With the backdrop of a £5m debt, which was costing the club £1,000 a week in interest, it wasn't going to be easy to find a new number one. On 28 October 1995 Jim sprung a surprise by naming a former French international in goal against Falkirk at Brockville. The man in question was the experienced 32-year-old Gilles Rousset. The towering Frenchman had started his career with Sochaux in 1982. He moved to Lyon in

1990 where he quickly established himself as their first choice, playing 98 matches over the next three seasons. During this period, Rousset was capped twice by France and was selected for the squad for the 1992 European Championship. He didn't, however, brush shoulders with Henry Smith who was also in Sweden with Scotland. He is very proud of representing his country and still has his two shirts he wore in the games against Kuwait in 1990 and England in 1992. As a young boy Gilles would never have thought he would play at a European Championship as a goalkeeper. He wanted to score goals like his hero Gordon McQueen, having watched him and admired the rest of the Leeds United team that he followed as a lad. However, when the regular stopper for his local boys' club didn't turn up for a game, Gilles agreed to step in and almost instantly realised that was the position for him as did the coach.

In 1993 Rousset transferred to Marseille, at the time the reigning champions of Europe. However, due to the presence and excellent form of a certain rising star named Fabien Barthez, Rousset did not manage a competitive start for the European giants. He then spent the next season with Rennes before his move to Hearts.

His debut would see a 2-0 defeat. The first goal against him in Scottish football was scored by David Weir, who would later become a trusted team-mate and fellow Scottish Cup winner. When I spoke to Gilles, he reminisced about his debut. Alan Rae, the Hearts physio, could speak a little French and asked Gilles about his preferred shirt colour for the game. Gilles mentioned he disliked playing in yellow as his previous team, Sochaux, predominantly wore that colour. He also wasn't fond of light or sky blue, considering it unlucky from past experiences. You can almost guess what options were offered to Rousset! His reaction upon hearing the choices was, 'F**k me!' Ultimately, he chose yellow, and it seemed to stick. Gilles was also aware that green was never an option, which suited him fine as his former team Lyon's biggest rivals, Saint-Étienne, played in green, a colour he never favoured.

Gilles's individual performances in the following months earned him widespread praise from fans, and the astute Jim Jefferies managed to convince him to stay until the end of the season. Gilles fondly recalls his first few months at the club, but one game stands out for him.

OUSS
SPL
SCOTTISH PREMIER LEAGUE

PONY
TENNENTS SCOTTISH CUP FINAL
1996
1874

He considers two saves from that match as among the best of his career. The game was a 0-0 draw at Fir Park against Motherwell. He laughed as he remembered the point-blank 'lucky' save from Paul Lambert, noting that he even had the audacity to hold on to the ball. Minutes later, he clawed away a ferocious 20-yard shot from Billy Davies that seemed destined for the back of the net. He felt that night galvanised both the fans and the team.

By then, Jim had strengthened his squad with new imports Hans Eskilsson and Pasquale Bruno, blending them with Scottish players, both young and old. The team began to climb the table slowly. Jim's mix of youth and experience led to rapidly improving results over the season and Hearts finished an impressive fourth, tied with Aberdeen on 55 points, and 32 points behind champions Rangers.

There was also the anticipation of a Scottish Cup Final against the formidable Rangers. Hearts were in high spirits, having already defeated Partick Thistle, Kilmarnock and St Johnstone before securing a famous Hampden win against Aberdeen in the semi-final. Notably, Hearts had never beaten Aberdeen in a Scottish Cup tie in their 122-year history. In the final, they had absolutely nothing to lose against the league champions. The progress that the team had made under Jim Jefferies and Billy Brown was there for all to see. However, the final was a one-sided affair and unfortunately a day to forget for Gilles. He had been in sparkling form throughout the season, but this would be the day that he made an error that would haunt him for a long time. In a rare error of judgement, he inexplicably let a low Brian Laudrup cross slip through his arms and legs for Rangers' second goal. John Colquhoun wrote about the final in his regular column in *Scotland on Sunday*, saying, 'Finally a word of consolation for our goalkeeper. Gilles Rousset has been a fantastic performer for Hearts, a friend to his team-mates and a hero to our supporters, and for this to happen to him in such a showcase occasion was almost like irony ploughing into tragedy.' So profoundly summed up by my boyhood hero.

In an interview with Sky Sports, Gilles admitted that after the game he was destroyed but said the fans had helped him get through the pain.

It's a massive understatement to say that the pain Gilles felt would ease massively come the final whistle of the 1998 Scottish Cup Final, after his pivotal role in the 2-1 defeat of Rangers. I can instantly recall some of his highlights on the day which included an acrobatic leap to palm away a Lorenzo Amoruso long-range effort in the first half, as well as a great stop at his right-hand post from Laudrup. The standout save in the second half was from Ally McCoist, when the ball dropped to him on the edge of the six-yard box but Gilles somehow managed to keep the ball out of the net much to the disbelief of the Scotland striker. Gilles even managed an assist when punting a free kick up to fellow Frenchman Stéphane Adam who latched on to it and shot past Andy Goram for Hearts' second goal.

Interviewed after the game, Gilles said to the press, 'Two years ago when we lost 5-1 in the final, we all felt very down. It was a particularly sore experience for me. Everyone in football makes mistakes and no one needed to tell me the one I made against Rangers was bad. This time was different and in spite of what happened before, I only went into the final with positive thoughts. He went on to add, 'I've played for my country at Wembley, but nothing compares with the experience of winning the cup with Hearts.' Gilles then finished off by saying, 'People have asked me about the McCoist save near the end of the match, but I don't remember too much about it. Maybe it was instinctive. What it felt like was a save made by the Hearts fans who were willing us to victory. It was 22,000 of us who pulled it off.' The last quote sums up what I and every Hearts fan felt in the dying minute of the game. What a day and what a performance by Rousset, never to be forgotten.

Pictured are a couple of shirts that have been worn by Gilles during his time at Hearts.

PONY

THIS SHIRT WAS WORN IN THE INFAMOUS SCOTTISH CUP FINAL AGAINST RANGERS IN 1996 AND WAS MANUFACTURED BY PONY.

The first shirt was worn in the infamous Scottish Cup Final against Rangers in 1996 and was manufactured by Pony. Pony was founded in 1972 by Uruguayan-born Roberto Muller, with financing from adidas chairman Horst Dassler. Pony stands for Product of New York. In the 90s the company designed shirts for Tottenham Hotspur, West Ham United and Coventry City. The Hearts keeper shirt features a traditional yellow body with black shoulders, collar, and sleeves. The shirt has a subtle design of very small squares entwined throughout. The Hearts badge is prominently placed in the centre of a maroon circle with black edging along with embroidered messaging around the badge that reads 'Tennent's Scottish Cup Final 1996'. Unlike the ten outfield players that day, this shirt did not feature the SPFL sleeve badges. The back of the shirt is completely black and displays the classic cloth-stitched Pony number. This top is part of the club's history and is remembered as a symbol of a significant era for Hearts.

The next shirt also reflects Gilles's preference for traditional, unfussy designs. It is from the 2000/01 season when his time at Hearts was nearing its end; he made eight appearances on the bench. By that time Hearts were wearing kits made by Erreà, an Italian sportswear company founded in 1988. This shirt has a black round-neck collar and cuffs. The centre of the body is yellow, with the sleeves and periphery in black, interspersed with a black pattern design and sporting the Bank of Scotland vinyl sleeve badges. The sponsor, Strongbow, is prominently displayed. The Erreà logo is positioned just under the centre of the collar, with a large Hearts crest below it. Sporting ID numbers and name set adorn the back of the shirt.

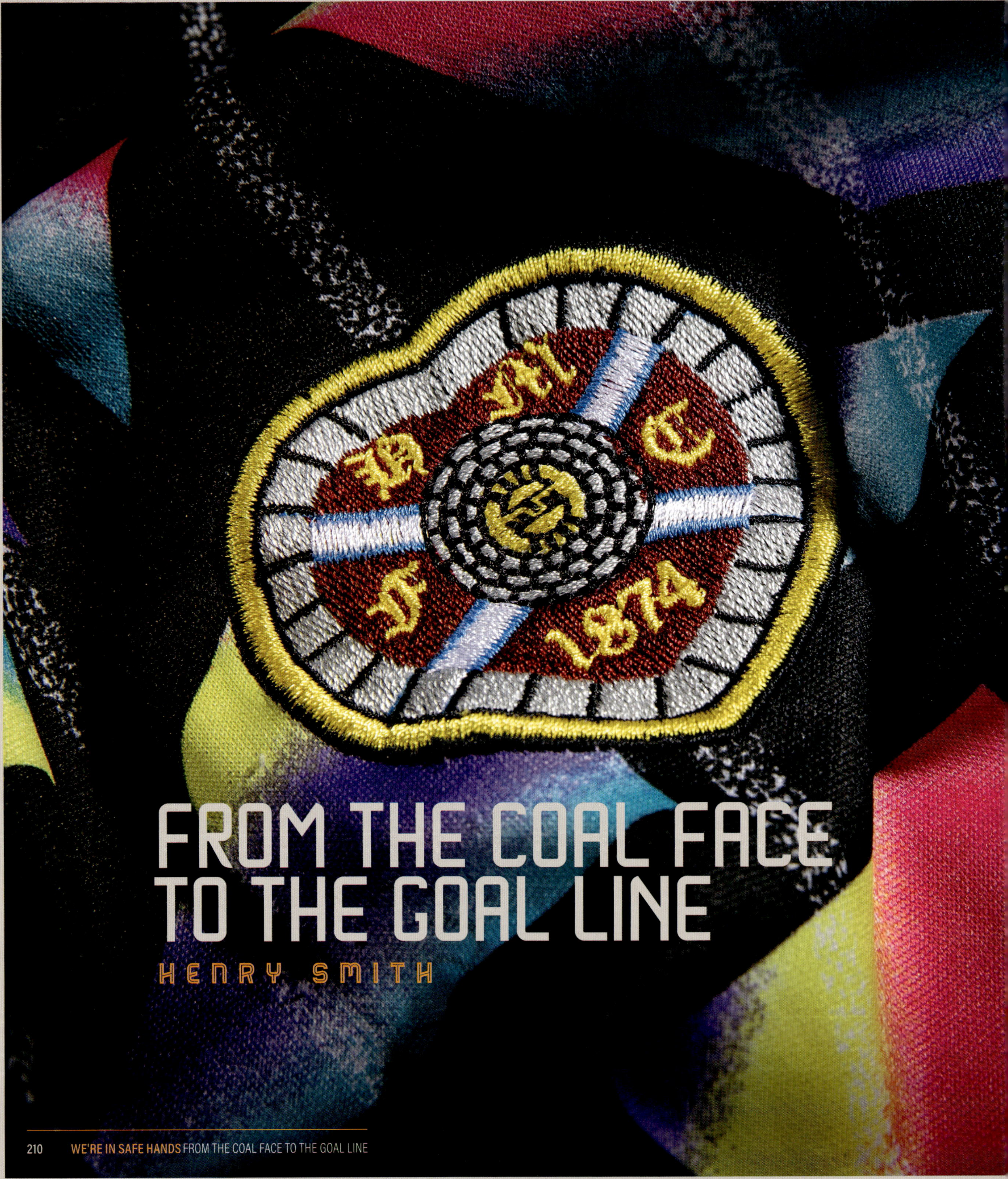

FROM THE COAL FACE TO THE GOAL LINE

HENRY SMITH

1988/89 – 1993/94

Henry Smith made an incredible 598 competitive appearances for Hearts in his 14 years at the club. Broken down, that was 476 league games, 45 Scottish Cup ties, 55 in the League Cup and 22 in Europe. If you add in the non-competitive matches, the total times Henry wore a Hearts shirt was 700. That really is an amazing number of games for one club. Only Gary Mackay (640) and John Robertson (632) have made more for Hearts. Henry kept 214 clean sheets which equated to 35.79 per cent of games played. He managed to save 12 of the 58 penalties that he faced.

I managed to spend time with Henry and one of the first things I was dying to ask him was to name his three favourite saves during his Hearts career. He was very quick to answer and mentioned one against Aberdeen on a Wednesday night at a rain-swept Tynecastle on 30 October 1985. Hearts led 1-0 thanks to Craig Levein and in the dying seconds of the game, he produced a miraculous stop from Neil Simpson. The perfectly placed shot from 14 yards out was deftly turned round for a corner. He loved that save as it was what he practised day in and day out during training. That save secured Hearts' first win in the league against Aberdeen in seven years.

The second was a save from Dundee United's Maurice Malpas, again in 1985/86. A huge Hearts support headed to Tannadice on 12 April, hoping that the incredible winning streak would continue and help edge the club towards a first top-division title win since 1959/60. It is a save that the fans in the crowd that day will remember. With Hearts holding a 1-0 lead thanks to a ferociously struck shot from outside the box by goal

machine John Robertson, Smith pulled off an out-of-this-world save from Malpas. Henry was unsighted when Malpas struck a perfect right-footer that the keeper kept out by twisting quickly to his right and pulling off a stop which was in the near miraculous category. The save changed the direction of traffic, inspiring the Men in Maroon to go on and win the game 3-0. Sandy Clark scored the second goal with Robbo adding his second of the game to round off the scoring. That win would mean Hearts would rewrite the record books with an unbeaten run of 29 games. On that run they had taken 42 points from a possible 50 since 5 October. Eight straight wins in league and cup produced a goals tally of 20 for and four against. Hearts also would not concede more than one goal in a league match after 21 September. Ultimately the season would end in disappointment but on reflection decades later, it was an absolute pleasure to watch that team play.

Then there was 'that' save from Tommy Coyne against Celtic in the league game on 16 November 1991. Anyone who saw it will recall the sheer athleticism of Smith: the way he transferred his body weight from left to right, twisted and turned changing direction, then got his hand to the ball and tipped it over the bar. With Hearts 1-0 down from a Coyne goal on 14 minutes, the save lifted the team and the crowd and they went on to win 3-1. The goalscorers were George Wright, Craig Levein and Scott Crabbe. An amazing save and an amazing game.

Henry then recalled his best 90 minutes in a Hearts shirt, a 0-0 draw against St Mirren on a gloomy and rainy Wednesday night on 30 October 1991. In difficult conditions he felt he played an almost flawless game, collecting crosses and holding any shots fired at him from distance or close range. The papers agreed, giving him a rating

BUKTA

of five stars out of five with only a one-word description alongside – 'unbeatable'. Guðmundur Torfason was the man who caused the most angst during the game, peppering Henry's goal from distance in exceedingly difficult conditions, but Smith and Hearts stood firm.

Smith was passed over by Barnsley as a 15-year-old, with the club deeming him 'too small'. He thought his chance of becoming a professional footballer might never happen and ended up following in his father's footsteps, going down the coal mine in Kirby for three years. At the same time, Henry was playing for local amateur teams. In 1978, after an impressive trial at Sunderland, he was offered a deal with the Black Cats under manager Jimmy Adamson. Rather than signing on the spot, he took the contract home as he wanted to take his dad's advice. After driving straight home to give his father the good news, he was greeted by his dad at the door, who told Henry he had to phone Adamson right away. On the phone, Jimmy explained that he had accepted an offer from Leeds United to become their manager and that he wanted Henry to come to Elland Road with him on the exact same terms as the Sunderland contract. Henry jumped at the chance.

He joined veteran keeper and former Scottish international David Harvey, as well as David's backup, youngster John Lukic. The Englishman would go on to play first-team football with Leeds and Arsenal. The Leeds team that Smith joined contained household names such as Trevor Cherry and Bryan Flynn, as well as Frank and Eddie Gray.

Henry stayed at Leeds until the summer of 1981 having found it hard to oust Lukic and was coming to the end of his contract with the club. This was when Heart of Midlothian came knocking at the Scotsman's door; club secretary Les Porteous asked him to come on trial during their pre-season tour of the north-east of England, in which Hearts would play against North Shields, Whitley Bay and Blyth Spartans.

Smith replaced John Brough at half-time during the first game of the tour, against North Shields, and from that moment on he never looked back. Wallace Mercer

took advice from *Evening News* journalist Stewart Brown, who was also at that game, and signed the 25-year-old on a full-time contract. Stewart thought Henry, at 6ft 2in, was impressive at commanding his area and dealing with high balls. Henry would be part of the Alex MacDonald revolution, which would see seismic changes in the club's fortunes. It is fair to say over the next decade that Henry would become one of the most popular players at Hearts. He would epitomise what the club was all about: team ethics, hard work in training and on the football pitch.

Henry would play an incredible 195 games on the trot from the end of March 1982, when Hearts won 3-0 at Raith Rovers.

One of Henry's favourite periods was the Euro run, which would end up seeing Hearts play European giants Bayern Munich at Tynecastle. That run would see something very unusual happen: he went off with an injury. He was involved in a clash on 80 minutes, which would see him require stitches in a nasty gash on his right shin. The injury meant substitute keeper Murray McDermott would make his one and only competitive appearance for the club. McDermott sadly passed away in 2003 at the age of 53. He played 494 games for Raith Rovers between 1970/71 and 1980/81 and was inducted into the Rovers Hall of Fame in 2016. Hearts would play against Austria Vienna, Velež Mostar and then Bayern Munich during that run.

Henry recalled his memories of both legs of the Bayern tie. He particularly remembered the away dressing room which appeared to have a swimming pool in it. This turned out to be the bath! He also talked about Klaus Augenthaler's goal, which would see Bayern take the lead with a shot which no keeper would have a chance of saving. Indeed, as the ball flew through the air, he knew he wasn't getting to it.

In another European adventure, when Hearts played Bologna at Tynecastle, Henry ended up in the police station. When Hearts scored, he turned round to the 30 away fans and gave them a famous Scottish gesture. The officials reported Henry to the police, and he had to visit Torphichen station with Les Porteous on the Thursday morning. He was let off with a warning.

HMFC
1874

Henry was inducted into the Hearts Hall of Fame in 2009. The description of his career ends with the following sentence, 'He was one of the finest goalkeepers ever to appear for Hearts and it would be impossible to calculate how many times Henry has turned a game in our favour.' For me, this encapsulates what Henry meant to me and to Hearts fans who were lucky enough to see him play.

Henry showed his mental strength during several seasons when Joe Jordan took charge and made it clear that Nicky Walker was going to be his first choice. Unfortunately for Nicky, he fractured his cheekbone exceedingly early in his time with Hearts, which meant Henry was back between the sticks. Smith kept Walker out of the side with his impressive form.

When Henry's career was winding down at Clydebank, he crossed paths with a young Craig Gordon who was on loan at Cowdenbeath, and the two sides met in the league. On 19 September 2001, when Clydebank beat Cowdenbeath 3-2, Craig saved a penalty but Alex Burke netted the rebound. Henry was on the winning side, which included Derek Ferguson and Barry Lavety.

Smith's career also included stints with Ayr United, Clydebank and Berwick Rangers before retiring.

When it came to shirts he wore, his favourites were the psychedelic shirts of the 90s, as he felt they matched his personality – colourful and entertaining.

The first shirt featured is a Bukta production. It has a grey body and features matching black collar and cuffs, as well as black patches running from the cuff to the elbows. Bukta sublimated their logo into the shirt, giving it a unique feel. The number also stands out with the word Bukta featuring vertically in the number itself. It has the Novafone sponsor which meant it was worn on or after the home league game against Rangers on 10 December 1989 as this was the first time the sponsor appeared on the shirts.

Hearts wore Admiral kits during the 1991/92 and 1992/93 seasons. This keeper shirt from 1991/92 features Admiral's now famous and unique flame

design, both distinctive and eye-catching. The flame effect typically used contrasting colours such as red, orange, yellow and blue, to create a vibrant and dynamic look. This design was not exclusively for keeper shirts; Southampton's away and third kits also featured the flame.

Henry's shirt was the blue version, with black shoulders, cuffs and collar trimmed in red. The shirt features the Admiral logo on the left, accompanied by the letters 'GK'. The right side features the Hearts crest. On the back is the unique black Admiral number in felt. This shirt is the same version that Henry was wearing when he made the save against Tommy Coyne.

In 1993/94 the club were wearing Asics. This shirt is a bright Asics template. This is a replica away version, but I like this shirt so much I wanted to feature it in the book. It's a typically bright, eye-catching design from Asics with the body of the shirt made up of small squares cut into yellow and grey diagonals. It has a black collar and cuffs with the black also running from the neck to the shoulders. It also features the Strongbow sponsor. Blackburn Rovers, Newcastle and Aston Villa wore the same shirt that season. Portsmouth wore the same template in grey/black.

Next is the home version from the same season. This is also an Asics template and was again also worn by Newcastle and Aston Villa. The shirt had a black round neck. The body and sleeves had random shapes such as squares, triangles and rectangles that were filled in with rainbow colours such as yellow, blue and pink, to name but a few. The sleeves also featured a black padded panel which ran from the shoulders to the elbow of the shirt. The sponsor would remain as Strongbow, with the logo heat-pressed flock appearing centrally on the shirt. The Asics logo and Hearts badge were embroidered. The number on the back was white stitched cloth.

Internationally, Smith earned three caps for Scotland between 1988 and 1992, playing against teams like Saudi Arabia, Northern Ireland and Canada. He was also part of the Scotland squad for Euro 92. Unfortunately, his international opportunities were limited due to the presence of other talented goalkeepers like Jim Leighton and Andy Goram. The Northern Ireland game

THE SCOTTISH FOOTBALL
ASSOCIATION

was particularly special for Henry as his dad was there to watch but would pass away a few weeks later. It meant the world to Henry that his dad got to see him play for Scotland.

He continued to reflect on his time with the national team, saying, 'David Bowman's dad Andy came up to me and said, "You'll play for Scotland one day." It was water off a duck's back; I assumed he was just being nice. Scotland did not really cross my mind. But I consistently played well, and that got me recognition with the Scotland squad. There were two certain keepers in Mr Goram and Mr Leighton, and those two did not make mistakes when they played for Scotland. I learned a lot by training with them and getting my personality over to them, showing what I could do. They basically couldn't live with me in training. I was in decent shape, really working my tail off, going in on a Sunday afternoon, where probably those two were out on the razz at night, which helped me a bit! Three caps I got because I worked my tail off, but I sat on the bench 27 times. Being involved in the squad was brilliant with the stars in those days.'

The last shirt is a Scotland top belonging to Henry. Known for his generosity towards Hearts supporters, he often donated his shirts for charity raffles and end-of-season supporter events. I sourced this from the original vendor who was the lucky raffle winner at the end of 1988/89. The Umbro shirt, which is deep red with navy and silver shoulder flashes, was typically paired with silver shorts. This bespoke shirt, launched in 1988 and worn until 1990, is a favourite among Scotland collectors.

Henry will be fondly remembered as a top keeper and a player who always gave 100 per cent for the jersey. A true Hearts Hall of Famer.

ACKNOWLEDGEMENTS

With thanks to: Davy Allan, Douglas Rankine, Jamie MacDonald, Zander Clark, Neil Alexander, Giles Rousset, Ian Westwater, Henry Smith, Mikey Mlotkiewicz, Aquapam, Nicky Walker, Mark Cairns, Jane Camillin, Ragnar Lochen, Ross Millar, Paul Mitchell, Duncan Olner, Chris Simm, Neil Strevens, Bill Alves, Alison Ross, Jim Ross, Gordon Paterson, Mary Paterson, Christine Peden, Graeme Porteous, Lloyd Porteous, Hearts Heritage, Craig Bryce, Dougie Bryce, Declan Bryce, Michael Logan, Carolyn Young, Luke Young.

CREDITS AND BIBLIOGRAPHY

www.londonhearts.com
www.oldfootballshirts.com
www.heartsfc.co.uk
www.olnerdesign.co.uk
www.scarvesaroundthefunnel.co.uk
www.umbro.com
www.truecoloursfootballkits.com
www.edinburgheveningnews.com
www.theglovebag.com
www.museumofjerseys.com
www.hmfkickback.co.uk
Hearts FC